PUBLIC HEALTH IN THE 21ST CENTURY

CAPACITY BUILDING

PLANNING, PROGRAMS AND PROSPECTS

PUBLIC HEALTH IN THE 21ST CENTURY

Additional books in this series can be found on Nova's website under the Series tab.

Additional e-books in this series can be found on Nova's website under the e-book tab.

PUBLIC HEALTH IN THE 21ST CENTURY

CAPACITY BUILDING

PLANNING, PROGRAMS AND PROSPECTS

DIANE BROWN
EDITOR

nova publishers
New York

NOTICE TO THE READER

Library of Congress Cataloging-in-Publication Data

Library of Congress Control Number: 2015953827

ISBN: 978-1-63483-995-2

Published by Nova Science Publishers, Inc. † New York

CONTENTS

PREFACE

The Patient Protection and Affordable Care Act (ACA) contains a provision that requires all nonprofit hospitals to conduct a Community Health Needs Assessment (CHNA) and an Implementation Plan every three years. The first chapter of this book provides a comprehensive analysis of the CHNA process, the priorities identified in the CHNA, and the implementation strategies produced by 31 small nonprofit rural hospitals in Nebraska. Chapter two discusses current capacity building mechanisms with community-based obesity programmes in the United Kingdom, revealing the importance of partnerships between multi-agencies involved in the process. Chapter three offers reflections on a Community-based participatory research (CBPR) project in partnership with the Latino migrant worker community in South Florida. Chapter four examines "KEQ" (Kapazitätsentwicklung im Quartier [Capacity Building in Residential Are-as/Neighborhoods]), which is the name of a newly developed questionnaire for measuring community capacities considered relevant to health. Chapter five discusses research on disaster recovery in several countries and the lessons learned regarding how personal, family, community and societal factors interact to facilitate adaptation to the consequences of disaster. The final chapter provides an overview of regional development planning, which is a conscious development strategy designed to bring about change and equity, and to improve the living standards of people by integrating economic, social and environmental policies and programmes in a spatial context.

Chapter 1 – The Patient Protection and Affordable Care Act (ACA) contains a provision that requires all nonprofit hospitals to conduct a Community Health Needs Assessment (CHNA) and an Implementation Plan every three years. This chapter provides a comprehensive analysis of the CHNA process, the priorities identified in the CHNA, and the implementation strategies produced by the 31 small nonprofit rural hospitals in Nebraska. Of these 31 hospitals, 30 are classified as critical access hospitals. The majority of the hospitals in the study worked closely with the local health department in their area and this partnership appeared to enhance the quality of the CHNA (e.g., the data analysis, input from the community and the priority setting process). The highest rated priorities among these 31 hospitals were: (1) access to care, (2) obesity, (3) mental health and substance abuse, and (4) cancer. There were also several specific strategies that were recommended to address these issues. Most of these strategies involved some type of education, increasing or adding new services, developing or implementing a new program, expanding health events or screenings, and expanding staff or providers. The chapter also includes several lessons learned and some key success factors. One of the lessons learned is that it is very important for small hospitals to work closely with their local health department and to align the CHNA with other plans in the area. By involving more partners, it is possible to design interventions that are broader in scope and have a greater collective impact in addressing the complex problems that were identified as the high priorities.

Chapter 2 – In recent years large community-based obesity prevention programmes have been developed in a number of Western countries in an attempt to reduce the growing epidemic of obesity in children and adults. The construction of community-based programmes revolves around the concept of capacity building. Often described as the 'invisible work' in health promotion, capacity building first establishes what structural limitations exist to prevent adoption of healthier lifestyles in communities, with a view to empowering community members to establish healthy behaviours. Typically, programmes attempt to address the main determinants of obesity by deploying an array of interventions at community level. Programmes frequently involve multiple stakeholders; for example, in England, programmes often involve local cross-government departments and networks of organisations acting as partners through a multi-agency approach. The strength of health promotion initiatives relies on formed 'coalitions' or partnerships and the subsequent collaboration in the design, delivery and administration of the programme's multiple components. Advantages of partnership are the pooling of resources, avoiding duplication and potentially understanding the social context more holistically given the engagement of stakeholders' from different perspectives. Despite best intentions, these large community-based programmes are not without difficulties and recent literature exposes stakeholder concerns particularly in relation to the development, implementation and evaluation of such programmes (Middleton et al. 2014, Kleij et al. 2015). This includes leadership issues, competing agendas and priorities, the unwieldy nature of large multi-agency networks and the complexities around making a sustained impact. Those involved in the administration of community-based obesity prevention programmes should carefully consider the components which lead to facilitation of efficiency in the capacity building process discussed in this commentary.

Chapter 3 – Despite an growing array of efficacious interventions tailored to immigrant and migrant populations in the US, there are mounting challenges in developing strategies that prevent and control HIV and other sexually transmitted infections (STIs), and that can be sustained and scaled to meet the needs of those most vulnerable to their impact. Community-based participatory research (CBPR) has received increasing recognition as a public health paradigm that combines epidemiology and behavioral science in order to understand how multiple determinants interact to influence health in a particular community. CBPR requires an equitable partnership between researchers and those directly affected by and knowledgeable of the local circumstances that impact health in a given community. Tangible, lasting health benefits require a balance of rigorous research that respectfully, productively, and equally involves community partners.

In this chapter, we offer our reflections on a CBPR project in partnership with the Latino migrant worker community in South Florida. We first discussed how we forged a partnership (known in the community as Project Salud) between researchers and community members. Next, we present the results and evaluate the efficacy of a community-based intervention to reduce risk behaviors and enhance mediators of HIV-preventative behaviors. Finally, we attempt to discuss some of the challenges inherent in CBPR and reflect on the question, “is CBPR a good fit?” We aim for our analysis to contribute a unique perspective to the rich, ongoing discussion about developing community capacity as a means to promote health, ameliorate health disparities, and promote justice in marginalized, vulnerable communities.

Chapter 4 – *Introduction:* “KEQ” (Kapazitätsentwicklung im Quartier [Capacity Building in Residential Areas/Neighborhoods]) is the name of a newly developed questionnaire for measuring community capacities considered relevant to health. It is particularly based on the preliminary work of Glenn Laverack and Ronald Labonte who originally differentiated between nine domains of community capacities. KEQ is the first measurement instrument for capacity building in Germany, and can be seen as an intermediate outcome parameter for health promotion programs and activities at the community-level. This research was funded by the Federal Ministry of Education and Research.

Objectives: The general research goal was the development of an instrument for the long-term assessment of health promotion activities in disadvantaged neighborhoods. This chapter will start presenting the neighborhood and health promotion program as the context for developing the instrument. The major section will focus on the psychometric testing of the KEQ instrument according to the classical test theory (objectivity, reliability, and validity). Practicality was analyzed in terms of length of time taken to complete the questionnaire, and number of missing values.

Methods: Surveys were conducted to measure community capacities, each with 40 to 60 stakeholders or change agents, from five socially disadvantaged areas in Hamburg, Germany, at different points in time. The KEQ instrument consists of five domains (participation, local leadership, available resources, networking and cooperation, health care) as a 51 item long-form. (A 31 item short-form is currently under development.) Analyses comprised both descriptive and inference statistics.

Results: Psychometric findings on the basis of N=235 respondents (37% out of 638 in total) permit the application of KEQ in small urban communities (about 3,000 to 20,000 residents). Cronbach's alpha as a coefficient of internal consistency ranged between .82 ("available resources") and .94 ("health care"). The results of the five domains of community capacity and their changes over time can best be depicted in spider diagrams. This form of presentation proved to be highly suitable for feed-back to agents of change in the residential areas involved.

Conclusion: The modular design of the questionnaire allows its flexible use for various assessment goals. Supposedly it is more suitable for measuring quality development than for evidence-producing outcome evaluation. Additional approaches are required to compensate for the possibly one-sided expert perspectives in the KEQ assessments (e.g., "triangulation" or "cross-examination" using groups of residents as informants). Further research is needed to study capacity building in association with final health outcomes.

Chapter 5 – In locations that expose citizens to large scale disasters, a key disaster risk reduction (DRR) goal is developing their adaptive capacity. The atypical nature of disasters make it important to understand how people, individually and collectively, adapt when experiencing disaster. This chapter discusses research on disaster recovery in New Zealand (2011 Christchurch earthquake), Taiwan (1999 Chi Chi earthquake) and Australia (2013 Tasmanian wildfire) and the lessons learnt regarding how personal, family, community and societal factors interact to facilitate adaptation to the consequences of disaster.

Data from the 2011 Christchurch earthquake and 1999 Chi Chi earthquake were obtained as survivors confronted the demands of disaster recovery. By collecting data from the 2013 Tasmanian wildfire using a Facebook page (Tassie Fires – We Can Help) specifically developed to assess response and recovery, the chapter offers rare in situ, real-time insights into adaptive demands and adaptive responses. These analyses are used to provide insights into adaption, and how models and theories of capacity building can be developed from such experience to inform the planning and design of capacity building programs. By conducting this work in countries that differ extensively in their cultural characteristics (comparing Taiwan and Australia/New Zealand), the chapter affords an opportunity to develop understanding of how cultural similarities and differences inform how capacity is developed, sustained and enacted.

Chapter 6 – In locations that expose citizens to large scale disasters, a key disaster risk reduction (DRR) goal is developing their adaptive capacity. The atypical nature of disasters make it important to understand how people, individually and collectively, adapt when experiencing disaster. This chapter discusses research on disaster recovery in New Zealand (2011 Christchurch earthquake), Taiwan (1999 Chi Chi earthquake) and Australia (2013 Tasmanian wildfire) and the lessons learnt regarding how personal, family, community and societal factors interact to facilitate adaptation to the consequences of disaster. Data from the 2011 Christchurch earthquake and 1999 Chi Chi earthquake were obtained as survivors confronted the demands of disaster recovery. By collecting data from the 2013 Tasmanian wildfire using a Facebook page (Tassie Fires – We Can Help) specifically developed to assess response and recovery, the chapter offers rare in situ, real-time insights into adaptive demands and adaptive responses. These analyses are used to provide insights into adaption, and how models and theories of capacity building can be developed from such experience to inform the planning and design of capacity building programs. By conducting this work in countries that differ extensively in their cultural characteristics (comparing Taiwan and Australia/New Zealand), the chapter affords an opportunity to develop understanding of how cultural similarities and differences inform how capacity is developed, sustained and enacted.

In: Capacity Building
Editor: Diane Brown
ISBN: 978-1-63483-995-2

Chapter 1

BUILDING COMMUNITY CAPACITY TO IMPROVE POPULATION HEALTH THROUGH INTEGRATING PUBLIC HEALTH AND HEALTH CARE: LESSONS LEARNED FROM THE COMMUNITY HEALTH NEEDS ASSESSMENT CONDUCTED BY NEBRASKA'S RURAL HOSPITALS

Li-Wu Chen*[*], MHSA, PhD, David Palm, PhD and Kate E. Trout, MPH

Department of Health Services Research and Administration, College of Public Health, University of Nebraska Medical Center, Omaha, Nebraska, US

ABSTRACT

The Patient Protection and Affordable Care Act (ACA) contains a provision that requires all nonprofit hospitals to conduct a Community Health Needs Assessment (CHNA) and an Implementation Plan every three years. This chapter provides a comprehensive analysis of the CHNA process, the priorities identified in the CHNA, and the implementation

---

[*] Corresponding author: Li-Wu Chen. E-mail: liwuchen@unmc.edu.

strategies produced by the 31 small nonprofit rural hospitals in Nebraska. Of these 31 hospitals, 30 are classified as critical access hospitals. The majority of the hospitals in the study worked closely with the local health department in their area and this partnership appeared to enhance the quality of the CHNA (e.g., the data analysis, input from the community and the priority setting process). The highest rated priorities among these 31 hospitals were: (1) access to care, (2) obesity, (3) mental health and substance abuse, and (4) cancer. There were also several specific strategies that were recommended to address these issues. Most of these strategies involved some type of education, increasing or adding new services, developing or implementing a new program, expanding health events or screenings, and expanding staff or providers. The chapter also includes several lessons learned and some key success factors. One of the lessons learned is that it is very important for small hospitals to work closely with their local health department and to align the CHNA with other plans in the area. By involving more partners, it is possible to design interventions that are broader in scope and have a greater collective impact in addressing the complex problems that were identified as the high priorities.

INTRODUCTION

The passage of the Patient Protection and Affordable Care Act (ACA) in 2010 created new opportunities to focus on population health (Patient Protection and Affordable Care Act 2010). The goal of population health is to improve the health outcomes of a group of individuals, including the distribution of such outcomes (Kindig and Stoddart 2003). Achieving this goal will require less emphasis on "sick care" and treatment and more emphasis on prevention, including addressing behavioral risk factors (e.g., tobacco and substance use, physical inactivity, and poor nutritional practices) and the social and environmental determinants of health (e.g., poverty levels, water quality, and the availability of housing). Improving the health of the population also requires a higher level of collaboration between health care providers (hospitals and physicians) and local public health agencies and other community-based organizations. To improve health outcomes and build more integrated systems of care between health care providers and public health agencies, the ACA included a provision that requires all nonprofit hospitals to conduct a Community Health Needs Assessment (CHNA) every three years. The CHNA must describe the community served, identify existing resources, and determine the highest priority needs.

These hospitals must also develop an Implementation Plan that contains specific strategies to address the priority needs that were included in the CHNA (Patient Protection and Affordable Care Act, Section 9007, 2010). This process provides hospitals with an opportunity to broaden their mission and to work more closely with public health agencies.

The purpose of this chapter is to provide a comprehensive analysis of the CHNA process, the priorities identified in the CHNAs, and the implementation strategies produced by the 31 small nonprofit rural hospitals in Nebraska. Among the 31 hospitals, 30 were Critical Access Hospitals (CAHs). CAHs were created by Congress under the 1997 Balanced Budget Act. This new designation was intended to improve the financial viability of rural hospitals and maintain access to health care services for rural residents. In order to receive cost-based reimbursement for services provided to Medicare patients and in some states Medicaid patients, CAHs are required to have no more than 25 inpatients beds, maintain an average length of stay of 96 hours in one fiscal year for acute care patients, provide emergency care 24-hours, seven-days a week, and be located in a rural area that is 35 miles from another hospital or receive a special designation from the state (Balanced Budget Act of 1997, 1997).

This chapter is divided into seven sections. The first section provides a general overview of the CHNA and Implementation Plan requirements that are contained in the ACA and the final rules issued by the Internal Revenue Service (IRS). The second section includes a description of the methods we used to collect and analyze the data and information. The third section examines the role of local health departments in the CHNAs and the level of collaboration between these departments and the hospitals. In the fourth section, the priorities included in all of the CHNAs are analyzed. The fifth section summarizes the intervention strategies that are included in the Implementation Plans. The sixth section discusses some of the lessons learned and key success factors for conducting CHNAs. The final section concludes this chapter.

Overview of the ACA Requirements

Based on the final rules released by the Internal Revenue Service (IRS), there are several areas that must be addressed in the CHNA (Federal Register 2014). One of the requirements is a description of the geographic area served. Since this analysis is limited to small rural hospitals, most of their patients reside in the county in which the hospital is located. This description should also include demographic and socioeconomic data. A second requirement is to identify the stakeholders that were involved in the CHNA process. Ideally, a broad-based coalition should be formed that includes representatives from the hospital, the business community, the schools, the faith community, nonprofit organizations, and the local health department. If the local health department does not participate, their staff must be consulted during the process. Input must also be received from persons who represent the broad interests of the community (i.e., medically underserved populations). This input could be obtained through focus groups or key informant interviews or town hall meetings.

A third requirement is to describe the process that was used to conduct the CHNA. Although a particular process was not specified, information should be examined through both quantitative and qualitative analysis. The quantitative analysis involves examining various types of data which may include the leading causes of death, the results of a local or regional behavioral risk factor survey, cancer registry data, hospital discharge data, and perhaps the County Health Rankings prepared annually by the University of Wisconsin (University of Wisconsin Population Health Institute 2015). The qualitative analysis is generally based on information obtained from focus groups, key informant interviews, or town hall meetings.

Another requirement of the CHNA is to list the needs that were identified and describe the criteria that were used to set the priorities. Although the law and subsequent regulations do not specify the criteria, most hospitals take into consideration the (1) the burden, (2) the severity or urgency of the health need, (3) the feasibility and effectiveness of potential interventions, and (4) the importance the community places on addressing the need.

Finally, the CHNA should address the resources that are available to meet the priority needs. These resources should include the medical services provided by the hospital and other health-related services that are available in the community (e.g., primary care, dental care, long-term care, pharmacy, emergency medical services (EMS), mental health and substance abuse, social services, and public health). When the CHNA is completed, it must be placed on the hospital's website and remain there until two subsequent CHNAs have been completed. If a hospital fails to meet the CHNA requirements, the hospital will be assessed an excise tax of $50,000 (Federal Register 2014).

The Implementation Plan must describe how the hospital will address each significant need that was identified in the CHNA. The plan is required to include the actions and activities the hospital intends to take and the potential impact of these actions. In addition, it must document the resources the hospital plans to commit and any planned collaborations between the hospital and other organizations in addressing the need. Finally, it must explain the reasons why the hospital is not addressing a significant need (Federal Register 2014).

METHODS

This study focuses on rural communities and includes the 31 small nonprofit rural hospitals (including 30 CAHs) in Nebraska. The only non-CAH that was included in our study sample is also a small rural hospital with less than 50 beds. This focus provides a unique perspective because rural areas have different demographic characteristics (e.g., a higher proportion of people over 65 years of age) and several different health care needs (e.g., access to health care issues, lower cancer screening rates, and a larger percentage of the population overweight or obese). Because CAHs have fewer resources and less community planning expertise, it also provides an opportunity to assess the relationship between hospitals and local health departments.

In this study, we obtained the CHNAs and implementation plans primarily from the hospital websites. In a few instances, a follow up telephone call was used to identify the link or obtain more complete information on the implementation strategies. Although most hospitals completed their CHNA in 2013, a few hospitals finished them before or after this year (Table 1).

Table 1. The Year When the CHNA and Implementation Plan was Completed by Small Rural Nonprofit Hospitals in Nebraska

Year of CHNA and Implementation Plan completion	Number (%) of rural hospitals
2011	1 (3.2)
2012	5 (16)
2013	23 (74)
2014	1 (3.2)
2015	1 (3.2)
Total	31 (100)

[§]Analysis of CHNAs and Implementation Plans among 31 small rural hospitals in Nebraska.

Also, three hospitals provided more than one CHNA on their websites for different years. The most comprehensive CHNA with an implementation plan was selected for each hospital. Hospitals that collaborated with the same health departments most often had very similar methods sections and report structures. These similarities suggest that the local health department may have played a greater role in completing the CHNA than was specified in the documents.

THE DEVELOPMENT OF THE CHNAS AND THE ROLE OF LOCAL HEALTH DEPARTMENTS

Figure 1 indicates that almost all of the 31 small rural hospitals developed their CHNA in collaboration with the local health department in their area (n = 27/31; 87%). For 65% of the hospitals (n = 20/31), the local health department assumed the lead role in coordinating the CHNA process. Furthermore, the local health departments' role was more expansive than others for 8 of these 20 hospitals because this role included both preparing and writing of the CHNA. The local health department had a limited role in two CHNAs (6.5%), where local health department representatives only served on an advisory council. Four (13%) hospitals did not state that the local health department had a role in their CHNAs. Our analysis suggests that the majority of the 31 nonprofit rural hospitals in Nebraska worked closely with the local health department in their region to develop the CHNA. The local health department often assisted the hospitals in gathering and analyzing data, selecting the health priorities, developing and fostering collaboration among diverse groups of consumers and health care providers, and assisting with conducting the focus group interviews. This was a natural partnership because all of these departments had recently completed or were in the process of completing a five-year community health improvement plan (CHIP) which included an extensive data analysis, input from the community, specific priorities, and intervention strategies. The CHIP is one of the key prerequisites of achieving voluntary accreditation under the Public Health Accreditation Board (PHAB) (Public Health Accreditation Board Standards and Measures 2011). In addition, most of the rural hospitals lacked the resources and expertise to meet all of the CHNA requirements. In working collaboratively with hospitals, many local health departments applied a planning process called Mobilizing for Action through Planning and Partnerships (MAPP).

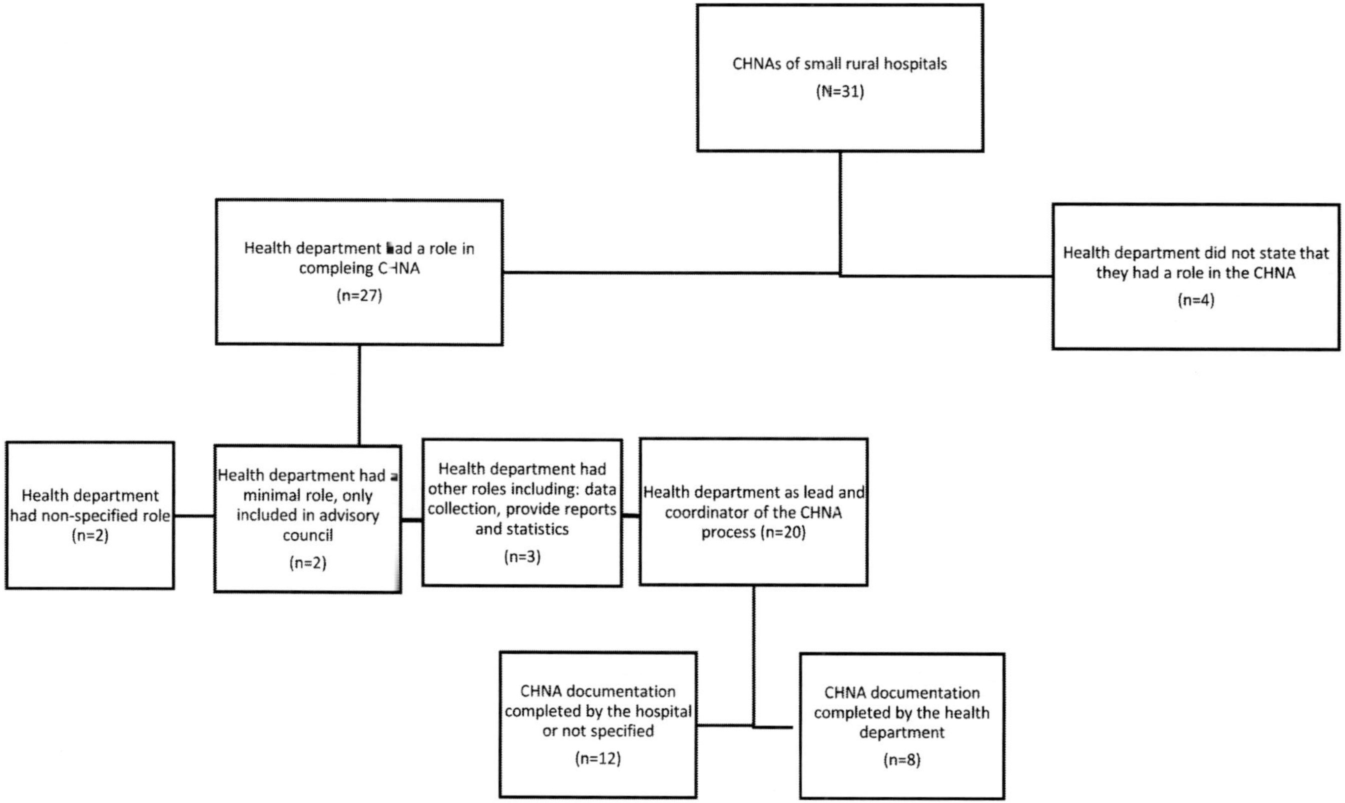

§Analysis of CHNAs and Implementation Plans among 31 small rural hospitals in Nebraska.

Figure 1. Role of the Local Health Department in Completing the Small Rural Hospital's CHNA in Nebraska.

This process consists of six major phases. The first phase is to organize a diverse coalition of stakeholders who will guide the planning process and become active partners during the implementation phase. The second phase is to develop a shared vision and common values. The third phase is to conduct a comprehensive needs assessment. In this phase a variety of quantitative and qualitative assessments are undertaken. For example, the health status assessment involves analyzing several databases, including birth data, mortality and morbidity data, behavioral risk factor data, the County Health Rankings, and others. It may also involve obtaining feedback directly from the community through a community themes and strengths survey and conducting focus group interviews.

After the needs have been identified, the coalition selects the most critical strategic issues that must be addressed to achieve the vision. Specific criteria are used to select the highest priority issues. These criteria may involve assessing the socio-economic impact, the likelihood that the issue can be changed, the capacity of the local health system to move this issue foreword, and the readiness or political will of the community to move foreword on this issue. The next phase is to formulate broad goals and develop strategies to achieve these goals.

In essence, an implementation plan is developed. The final phase is called the action cycle and involves moving foreword on the implementation plan. Ideally, the implementation activities will involve multiple partners and include an evaluation process to track progress over time (NACCHO 2015).

Data Collection Methods for CHNAs

Most of the hospitals used a variety of secondary data sources (n = 27/31; 87%), including the leading causes of death, infectious disease data, cancer registry data, hospital discharge data, birth data, and behavior risk factor data. In addition, the majority of hospitals conducted focus group interviews (n = 22/31; 71%).

Most of the focus group interviews were used to collect information about the most pressing health issues in the community. Several other methods were also used to obtain information from the community, including convening community meetings (e.g., community brainstorming meetings and "town-hall" style meetings), holding informal conversations with community leaders, generating an informal consensus in meetings among community stakeholders, using power point presentations to present information on key community health issues and asking the meeting participants to identify the highest priority issues, conducting key informant interviews, and collecting information informally in a day long public health workshop.

In 68% (n = 21/31) of the CHNAs, surveys were used as a source of information from their local population about important health issues. Among those surveys, 16 (76%) were in written forms, 12 (57%) were conducted using telephone, 10 (48%) were distributed via Internet (email or Survey Monkey), and only 8 (38%) utilized all three modes to maximize their response rate. Almost all of the local surveys were designed to collect community-level health data.

However, not all of these surveys were conducted by the rural hospitals or the local health departments. Several CHNAs included the results of a Community Themes and Strengths Survey conducted by the Nebraska Department of Health and Human Services. This survey was designed to obtain information about the most pressing health care needs in their communities and the sample size was large enough so that the data could be analyzed by the local health department regions.

Priorities Identified through CHNAs

In Tables 2 and 3, the high priority health needs identified by the 31 nonprofit rural hospitals are displayed. Table 2 shows the priorities that were ranked either one or two by the hospital. The highest rated priority was access to health care services where almost half of the hospitals (48%) rated this priority as top one or two.

At a minimum, access to care generally includes the availability of health care professionals and the ability to pay for health care services. Nebraska has several rural areas designated as Health Professional Shortage Areas (HPSAs) or Medically Underserved Areas (MUAs) for primary care health professionals, dentists, and mental health professionals. For example, almost half of the rural counties are classified as HPSAs or MUAs for primary care and all but three of the 93 counties in the state are designated as shortage areas for mental health (Nebraska DHHS 2014). Many rural areas also have an inadequate supply of many other types of health professionals, including nurses, physical therapists, and pharmacists. In addition, there are still many people in Nebraska who lack adequate health insurance coverage or do not have any health insurance. While the uninsured rate is relatively low at 11.3% (United Health Foundation 2014), it is estimated that almost 200,000 people do not have any health insurance coverage and many others have low-incomes but high deductible plans. These problems have been further magnified because many people who are eligible to obtain coverage through the health insurance exchange have not signed up.

The second highest priority that was frequently ranked top one or two by the hospitals was obesity. A total of 11 hospitals (35%) indicated that this issue was a serious problem for the community they serve. This ranking is not surprising given that adult obesity rates are rising rapidly according to the 2015 Nebraska Health Status Assessment.

In 2014, two-thirds of adults were either overweight or obese (SBSRC 2015). In rural areas, the obesity rates are above the urban rates (31.6% versus 27.5%) (SBSRC 2015). In addition, in the 2011 Community Themes and Strengths Assessment Survey, over 24% of the respondents listed overweight and obesity as the single most important health issue or health behavior that needs to be addressed in their community (Nebraska DHHS, April 2013). Alcohol abuse was rated as the second most important health issue at 8.6% in that survey.

The third highest priority that was frequently ranked top one or two was mental health and substance abuse. As previously mentioned, there is a serious shortage of mental health professionals in rural Nebraska. As a result, most mental health problems are diagnosed by family physicians. Many individuals are also reluctant to seek help for these conditions because of the stigma attached to mental illness. Inadequate or the lack of insurance coverage may also prevent some individuals from seeking timely care (Druss et al. 2001). According to the 2015 Nebraska Health Status Assessment, almost 16% of rural residents have been told they have depression and the suicide rates are the highest in the state (SBSRC 2015).

Substance abuse, especially alcohol misuse, has been a major problem in Nebraska for several years. Adult binge drinking rates in Nebraska have consistently exceeded the national average. In 2013, 20% of Nebraska adults indicated that they binge drank in the past 30 days as compared to the national rate of 16.8% (SBSRC 2015). During the period of 2011 to 2014, the rural rates for both binge drinking (23.5%) and drinking and driving (3.6%) were higher than their urban counterparts in the state (SBSRC 2015). Although prescription drug use is considerably below the national average, the rates are rising rapidly (Nebraska DHHS, August 2013). The fourth highest priority that was frequently ranked either top one or two was cancer which has recently overtaken heart disease as the leading cause of death in Nebraska.

Table 2. Number of Small Rural Nonprofit Hospitals that Ranked Specific Area as Top 1 or 2 Priority in Nebraska (N = 31)

Hospitals' Top 1 or 2 Priorities	
Specific Area	Number of Hospitals (%)
Access to Care	15 (48%)
Obesity	11 (35%)
Mental Health/Substance Use	9 (29%)
Cancer	8 (26%)
Diabetes	5 (16%)
Healthy Living	4 (13%)
Maternal and Child Health	2 (6.5%)
Heart Disease	1 (3.2%)
Family Issues	1 (3.2%)
Increase Physician Specialists	1 (3.2%)

[§]Analysis of CHNAs and Implementation Plans among 31 small rural hospitals in Nebraska.

Although urban death rates due to cancer are above rural death rates, rural residents were less likely to be screened for breast cancer and colon cancer.

For adults 18 and over, 79% of women living in urban areas had a mammogram during the period of 2011-2014 but the corresponding rate for women living in rural areas was 71%. During the same period, the urban and rural rates for colon cancer screening were 67% and 56%, respectively (SBSRC 2015).

There were also several other priorities that were frequently ranked top one or two, including diabetes, healthy living which generally included physical activity and good nutrition, and maternal and child health. None of these areas, however, had more than five hospitals that ranked them as a very high priority.

Table 3 shows the number (and percentage) of Nebraska's small rural nonprofit hospitals that listed a specific area as a priority overall. The top six priorities are mental health and substance abuse (81%), obesity (58%), access to care (55%), nutrition and physical activity (55%), cancer (45%), and healthy living (42%). Based on this list of priorities, it is obvious that mental health and substance abuse are considered major problems across the state. In addition, many hospitals are very concerned about the impact of obesity and its risk factors such as physical inactivity and poor nutrition on diabetes, heart disease, and cancer.

The priorities in Nebraska are remarkably similar to those identified in other studies. For example, based on the results of a 2014 survey conducted by the Association of American Medical Colleges (AAMC) of their member hospitals, the most frequent priority needs were: (1) access to care, (2) mental health, (3) obesity, (4) social determinants of health, (5) substance abuse, (6) physical activity and nutrition, and (7) health insurance coverage (AAMC 2014). Another recent study surveyed a total of 1,214 rural health stakeholders to identify the top 10 rural health priorities from among the national Healthy People 2020 priorities.

Based on the results of the survey, access to care which included emergency services, primary care, and insurance coverage was the highest rural priority. The next highest priorities in order of their ranking were: nutrition and weight status, diabetes, mental health and mental disorders, substance abuse, heart disease and stroke, physical activity and health, older adults, maternal and child health, and tobacco use (Bolin et al. 2015).

Table 3. Number of Small Rural Nonprofit Hospitals that Ranked Specific Area as a Priority Overall in Nebraska (N = 31)

Hospitals' Overall Priorities	
Specific Area	Number of hospitals (%)
Mental Health/Substance Use	25 (81%)
Obesity	18 (58%)
Access to Care	17 (55%)
Nutrition and Physical Activity	17 (55%)
Cancer	14 (45%)
Healthy Living	13 (42%)
Diabetes	11 (35%)
Heart Disease	6 (19%)
Injuries and Violence prevention	5 (16%)
Environment and Safety	5 (16%)
Aging Services	5 (16%)
Family Issues	5 (16%)
Maternal and Child Health	4 (13%)
Increase Physician Specialists	3 (9.7%)
Tobacco Prevention	2 (6.5%)
Dental Care	1 (3.2%)
Economic Growth	1 (3.2%)
Health Costs and Quality	1 (3.2%)

[§]Analysis of CHNAs and Implementation Plans among 31 small rural hospitals in Nebraska.

THE INTERVENTION STRATEGIES INCLUDED IN IMPLEMENTATION PLANS

Table 4 presents the strategies that were commonly identified by Nebraska's small rural nonprofit hospitals to address their high priority areas. The information was obtained directly from the hospital's implementation plans.

Table 4. The Common Strategies identified by Nebraska's Small Rural Nonprofit Hospitals to address their High Priority Needs

Strategies	Access to care (n* = 12) n (%)	Obesity (n* = 11) n (%)	Mental Health/ Substance Abuse (n* = 11) n (%)	Cancer (n* = 8) N (%)	Diabetes (n* = 3) n (%)
Education	9 (75)	11 (100)	11 (100)	8 (100)	3 (100)
Compile resources/services available	4 (33)	1 (9.1)	6 (55)	0	1 (33)
Expand hours	1 (8.3)	0	0	0	0
Expand staff/providers	3 (25)	1 (9.1)	9 (82)	2 (25)	0
Increase or add new services	8 (67)	3 (27)	8 (73)	5 (63)	1 (33)
Create a team	3 (25)	0	1 (9.1)	0	0
Plans to develop a new wellness center	0	2 (18)	0	0	0
Health events/screenings/ vaccinations	8 (67)	6 (55)	2 (18)	6 (75)	2 (67)
Apply for or expand funding	2 (17)	2 (18)	2 (18)	0	0
Develop/implement program	6 (50)	10 (91)	8 (73)	6 (75)	3 (100)
Develop/utilize tool	4 (33)	0	8 (73)	4 (50)	1 (33)
Use of Website/Internet	0	1 (9.1)	2 (18)	0	2 (67)
Utilize telehealth	5 (42)	0	4 (36)	4 (50)	0
Policy Development	0	6 (55)	6 (55)	0	1 (33)

§Analysis of CHNAs and Implementation Plans among 31 small rural hospitals in Nebraska.

*The sub-sample describes the hospitals' providing implementation plans for specific priority areas. Access to care (n = 12), 3 were excluded because of missing Implementation Plan; Obesity (n = 11); Mental Health/Substance Abuse (n = 11), 2 were excluded because of missing Implementation Plan; Cancer (n = 8) 1 was excluded because of missing Implementation Plan; Diabetes (n = 3), 2 were excluded because of missing Implementation Plan.

§Analysis of CHNAs and Implementation Plans among 31 small rural hospitals in Nebraska.

Figure 2. The Most Common Strategies Used by the Nebraska's Small Rural Nonprofit Hospitals to Address the Top Four Priorities.

A total of five hospitals did not identify any implementation strategies for their first or second priority and seven hospitals did not have an implementation strategy for its third priority.

Figure 2 displays the strategies that were most commonly used by Nebraska's small rural nonprofit hospitals to address the top four priorities (access to care, obesity, mental health and substance abuse, and cancer).

To address the issue of access to care, the majority of the rural hospitals used educational activities and programs (n = 9; 75%). These educational strategies included providing education on health care resources/services available in the community, increasing health education services, disseminating information of local initiatives to facilitate coordination of health care services, and facilitating education of Medicaid or federal subsidy eligibility for health insurance plans. The second most common strategy was to increase or add new services (n = 8; 67%), which involved providing weekly open lab days for blood screening at reduced rates, conducting physicals for Boy Scouts and firefighters, providing flu shots to businesses, providing concussion testing, increasing mammography screening, increasing other types of cancer screening, increasing preventive dental service and oral health care system, providing medication management assistance, and advising agencies about the implementation of Health Insurance Exchanges. The third most popular strategy was to organize health events/screenings/vaccinations in the community (n = 8; 67%). Five hospitals wanted to expand the use of telehealth services and six hospitals intended to develop and implement a new program (e.g., creating a volunteer transportation program for patients, developing a program to facilitate communication opportunities between providers and patients, and organizing worksite wellness programs). Only three hospitals that ranked this issue in the top three priorities suggested adding new staff and providers.

A total of four hospitals wanted to develop or use a new tool which included a central call line, an online patient portal, a resource directory, and automated health screening reminders as part of their electronic medical record. The two most common strategies for addressing obesity were educational programs and activities (n = 11; 100%) and developing and implementing new programs (n = 10; 91%). The educational programs involved offering bilingual education classes and healthy cooking courses, developing educational materials and courses to promote physical activity and nutrition, and providing obesity-related education through community messages, multi-media campaigns, and articles published via newspapers and/or websites. Some examples of the new programs included employee wellness programs, city-wide childhood obesity programs, programs for postpartum women, exercise programs, children's summer programs, wellness programs for small businesses and individuals, Farmers' Market programs, weekly after school physical activity programs, school-based programs, and programs promoting fitness for older generations. The third most common strategy was to develop new policies (e.g., limiting sugar and unhealthy foods; advocating for obesity prevention-related policies, educating elected officials about policy changes and community planning, design, and recreation, promoting school-related policies about more recess, and surveying local businesses to assess their readiness to initiate healthy policies).

The most common strategies for addressing mental health and substance abuse were focused on education (n = 11; 100%), including providing information of available resources, educating students on career opportunities in psychiatry/mental or behavioral health, developing school-based mental health awareness and educational programs, providing online screening and education, initiating community-based educational programs regarding behavioral health, providing education and awareness about the risks of prescription drugs, developing community-wide education plans, and developing programs that enhance self-advocacy skills, healthy relationships, and personal boundaries for adolescents. The second and third most common strategies were expanding staff and providers (n = 9; 91%) and increasing or adding new services (n = 8; 73%) (e.g., existing behavioral/mental health services, providing counseling two times a month, providing psychiatric consultations at nursing homes, identifying opportunities to expand counseling services, expanding telehealth services, assessing the feasibility of adding a specialty clinic in psychiatry, assisting other providers in becoming certified Medicaid/Medicare providers, and adding psychiatric capacity as part of a remote emergency Employee Assistance Program). Another strategy was to develop and implement a new program (n = 8; 73%), including developing an Employee Assistance Program in the school district, implementing an online option for an Employee Assistance Program, and adding a program that would allow employers to conduct drug testing on employees). Finally, eight (73%) hospitals indicated that they would develop or use a new tool such as a mental health resource database, a uniform screening tool to detect mental health problems such as depression and potential suicides, and prepare and implement a drug take back plan.

There were also several strategies related to cancer. The most common strategies mentioned in the implementation plans were education (n = 8; 100%), health events and screenings (n = 6; 75%), and develop and implement a new program (n = 6; 75%). The educational activities and new programs involved increasing cancer screenings, providing education on sun safety and skin cancer prevention, promoting general cancer awareness in the community, expanding disease registry programs, initiating a cancer of the month program to expand community education and screenings, promoting screening guidelines in other facilities, developing messages through a multi-media campaign to promote screening guidelines, and working with the public health system to align with other programs such as worksite wellness programs.

Lessons Learned and Key Success Factors

Based on the results of this study, it appears that nonprofit rural hospitals in Nebraska can successfully complete a CHNA and an implementation plan. However, some of the lessons learned and key success factors are discussed below. One of the key success factors is that it is advantageous for rural hospitals to work closely with the local health department in their area. Most of the local health departments in Nebraska have completed multiple needs assessments and community health improvement plans using the MAPP process. As a result, they have already complied and analyzed data, obtained input from their community through focus group interviews, town hall meetings, and/or community surveys. They also have experience in applying various criteria to select priorities, identifying and implementing evidence-based strategies, and tracking progress. As a general rule, we found that hospitals that had a strong partnership with their local health department had more complete plans.

Because most rural hospitals are located in areas that are very similar from a demographic, socioeconomic status, and health need standpoint, it is usually more advantageous to use regional data rather than county data. For example, the Behavior Health Risk Factor Surveillance System surveys are valid and reliable on a regional basis, but using the small numbers from a single county would usually not lead to statistically significant conclusions. Although mortality data are available on a county basis, the data would need to be aggregated over a large number of years to determine any significant trends. On the other hand, hospitals should carefully examine their hospital discharge data and it is critical to obtain input and feedback directly from people in the hospital's service area.

As expected, there appears to be a learning curve in developing the CHNA and the implementation plan. When multiple plans were available from the same hospital, in all cases the most recent plan was more comprehensive and included more targeted intervention strategies.

Although the vast majority of the CHNAs appeared to meet all of the IRS requirements, some of the plans lacked details about their data sources, data collection methods, and the analysis of the data. It would be helpful if all of the hospitals used a "core set" of indicators so there would be some standardization across the state. Of course, hospitals would always have the flexibility of including additional data and information.

Most of the significant gaps were in the implementation plans. In a few hospitals the strategies were not clear and it was very difficult to determine specifically what the role of the hospital would be, who the partners were, what the timeline was, what specific resources would be allocated, and how success would be measured. These limitations could easily be overcome with a detailed work plan that includes measureable objectives.

Without measureable objectives, it will be difficult if not impossible to evaluate the short-and long-term success of the strategies.

Some hospitals attempted to align their priorities with the local health department. There are several advantages to having a common set of priorities between the hospitals in the region and the local health department which are required by law to be regional in rural Nebraska. By combining resources and assets and involving other community partners, the interventions can be broader in scope and more targeted to address the unique needs of the region. Without this alignment, it will be nearly impossible for any single organization to be successful in addressing the problems of access to health care services, obesity, mental health and substance abuse, and cancer. These are complex issues which require a wide variety of intervention strategies.

CONCLUSION

This study has found that small rural hospitals can develop comprehensive CHNAs and implementation plans, and these documents can serve as a catalyst to improve the health of communities. However, to enhance the long-term effectiveness of these initiatives it is imperative to not only involve the local health department, but also many other community partners.

It is also important for state health agencies, colleges of public health, state hospital associations, and others to support these efforts by providing technical assistance, making data available at the local level, identifying evidence-based programs and practices, evaluating the CHNA process and the effectiveness of the implementation programs, and funding pilot programs that show great promise. Once successful strategies are identified, they can be replicated in other parts of the state.

REFERENCES

Association of American Medical Colleges (AAMC). (2014). *Community Health Needs Assessments: Engaging Community Partners to Improve Health*. Washington, DC: Alberti, P.M., Sutton, K.S., Baer, I., Johnson, J.

Balanced Budget Act of 1997, Pub. L. 105-33, 111 Stat. 251, (1997).

Bolin, J. N., Bellamy, G. R., Ferdinand, A. O., Vuong, A. M., Kash, B. A., Schulze, A. and Helduser, J. W. (2015). Rural Healthy People 2020: New Decade, Same Challenges. *The Journal of Rural Health.*

Druss, B. G., Marcus, S. C., Olfson, M., Tanielian, T., Elinson, L. and Pincus, H. A. (2001). Comparing the national economic burden of five chronic conditions. *Health Affairs*, 20(6), 233-241.

Federal Register. (2014). *Additional Requirements for Charitable Hospitals; Community Health Needs Assessments for Charitable Hospitals; Requirement of a Section 4959 Excise Tax Return and Time for Filing the Return*. Retrieved from http://federalregister.gov/a/2014-30525.

Kindig, D. and Stoddart, G. (2003). What is population health*? American Journal of Public Health*, 93(3), 380-383.

Nebraska Department of Health and Human Services (DHHS), Division of Public Health. (2013, April). *The Nebraska Public Health Improvement Plan: A Statewide Plan for Public Health Partners and Stakeholders to Improve the Health of Nebraskans*. Retrieved from http://dhhs.ne.gov/publichealth/Documents/SHIP%20Plan.pdf.

Nebraska Department of Health and Human Services (DHHS), Division of Public Health. (2013, August). *The Nebraska Statewide Health Needs Assessment*. Retrieved from http://dhhs.ne.gov/publichealth/Documents/2013%20Needs%20Assessment%20Final.pdf.

Nebraska Department of Health and Human Services (DHHS), Office of Rural Health. (December 4, 2014) *Office of Rural Health State and Federal Shortage Areas.* Retrieved from http://dhhs.ne.gov/publichealth/Pages/hew_orh_samaps.aspx.

Social and Behavioral Science Research Consortium (SBSRC). (2015). *Nebraska Health Status Assessment 2015*. Lincoln, NE: Hill, T. W., Espineli, J., Arneson, L., Knott, M. A. and Armitage, J.

Patient Protection and Affordable Care Act, 42 USC. § 18001 et seq. (2010).

Patient Protection and Affordable Care Act, 42 USC. § 9007, (2010).

Public Health Accreditation Board. (2011). *The Public Health Accreditation Board Standards and Measures version 1.0*. Retrieved from http://www.phaboard.org/wp-content/uploads/PHAB-Standards-and-Measures-Version-1.0.pdf.

The National Association of County and City Health Officials (NACCHO). (2007). *A strategic approach to community health improvement: MAPP field guide*. Washington, DC: National Association of City and County Health Officials.

United Health Foundation. (2014). *America's health rankings 2014*. Retrieved from www.americashealthrankings.org.

University of Wisconsin Population Health Institute. (2015). *County Health Rankings and Roadmaps*. Retrieved from www.countyhealthrankings.org.

In: Capacity Building
Editor: Diane Brown

ISBN: 978-1-63483-995-2

Chapter 2

COLLABORATION OR CONTESTATION? A CRITICAL EVALUATION OF CURRENT CAPACITY BUILDING MECHANISMS IN COMMUNITY-BASED OBESITY PREVENTION PROGRAMMES

G. Middleton[1,*], A. B. Evans[2], H. Henderson[1] and D. Windard[1]
[1]University of Lincoln, Brayford Campus, Lincoln, Lincolnshire, UK
[2]University of Copenhagen, København, Denmark

ABSTRACT

In recent years large community-based obesity prevention programmes have been developed in a number of Western countries in an attempt to reduce the growing epidemic of obesity in children and adults. The construction of community-based programmes revolves around the concept of capacity building. Often described as the 'invisible work' in health promotion, capacity building first establishes what structural limitations exist to prevent adoption of healthier lifestyles in communities, with a view to empowering community members to establish healthy behaviours. Typically, programmes attempt to address

---

* For author correspondence: gmiddleton@lincoln.ac.uk

the main determinants of obesity by deploying an array of interventions at community level. Programmes frequently involve multiple stakeholders; for example, in England, programmes often involve local cross-government departments and networks of organisations acting as partners through a multi-agency approach. The strength of health promotion initiatives relies on formed 'coalitions' or partnerships and the subsequent collaboration in the design, delivery and administration of the programme's multiple components. Advantages of partnership are the pooling of resources, avoiding duplication and potentially understanding the social context more holistically given the engagement of stakeholders' from different perspectives. Despite best intentions, these large community-based programmes are not without difficulties and recent literature exposes stakeholder concerns particularly in relation to the development, implementation and evaluation of such programmes (Middleton et al. 2014, Kleij et al. 2015). This includes leadership issues, competing agendas and priorities, the unwieldy nature of large multi-agency networks and the complexities around making a sustained impact. Those involved in the administration of community-based obesity prevention programmes should carefully consider the components which lead to facilitation of efficiency in the capacity building process discussed in this commentary.

The rising prevalence of obesity in developed countries has resulted in (Gortmaker et al. 2011, Wang et al. 2011) 'community-based,' 'population-based,' 'population-wide' or 'whole of the community' public health programmes being advocated as a preventative strategy (Simmons et al. 2009, Cecchini et al. 2010, King et al. 2011, WHO 2012). Theoretically, these population wide programmes aim to tackle obesity by targeting designated geographical segments (and their inhabitants) that are likely to be exposed to health inequalities, inhabit areas of multiple deprivation and have no prior screening risk (WHO 2004). The terms 'universal prevention' and 'primary prevention' are used to describe such population-based approaches (WHO 2004, Kumanyika et al. 2008, King et al. 2011). This commentary adds to the literature in this area, as the authors discuss current capacity building mechanisms with community-based obesity programmes in the United Kingdom, revealing the importance of partnerships between multi-agencies involved in the process.

There is an increasing body of research which has investigated community-based approaches to obesity prevention (for recent systematic reviews see Wolfenden et al. 2014 / Kleij et al. 2015). Implementation of CBOPs can be extremely appealing for Public Health practitioners and commissioners as the population-based programmes have potential to influence large numbers of local people with both health and social benefits (Wolfenden et al. 2014), attempting to tackle behaviours which promote weight gain across multiple settings (King et al. 2011). CBOPs also have the inherent capacity to address the various determinants of obesity in recognition of the complex aetiology of obesity (Wolfenden et al. 2014). Most CBOPs have been designed with regard to the social-ecological model of obesity (Economos and Irish-Hauser 2007, DeMattia and Denney 2008) and/or 'systems thinking' which has underpinned much of the contemporary effort to translate obesity science into policy areas (Allender et al. 2015).

A CBOP in England is usually designed to be responsible for large demographic segments identified as 'deprived populated areas' by a national index of multiple deprivation (Department of Communities and Local Government 2011). A programme contains a series of interventions which aim to address the main determinants of obesity (see Middleton et al. 2014). Interventions use a wide-range of activities that focus on changing nutrition and physical activity behaviours in the local community. Delivery is usually inclusive and flexible ensuring that interventions are equitable and meet community need. Ideally, existing communities, once involved in the programme, learn to take action, have ownership and even control some of the determinants of the unhealthy behaviours which promote weight gain.

This significantly differs in approach to more traditional expert-led or medical models of health promotion (Kumanyika et al. 2008, Naidoo and Willis 2009, Allender et al. 2011). Conceptually, the potency of CBOP is linked to the foundations on which potential interventions can be designed and delivered at community or ground-level (Wilson et al. 2009, Allender et al. 2011). Local capacity building is at the very foundation of CBOPs (as a framework) for community-based work or development, aiming to produce competent and skilled community people (Ballie et al. 2009, Liberato et al. 2011). Often described as the 'invisible work' behind health promotion (Davies and MacDowell 2006), capacity building is "the development of sustainable skills, organisational structures, resources and commitment to health improvement in health and other sectors to prolong and multiply health gains many-times over" (Hawe et al. 1997). This is viewed as central to public health intervention management and critical to the creation of supportive environments to facilitate long term healthy lifestyle changes (Ballie et al. 2009, Liberato et al. 2011).

To ensure that interventions meet the needs of the participants, members of the local community should be engaged in the decision-making processes throughout the design and implementation of such programmes (Kumanyika et al. 2008). Indeed, the level of engagement with local people can shape the nature of participation and implementation of the programme (Economos and Irish-Hauser 2007, King et al. 2011). Programmes have extensive settings including schools, children's centres, work sites, leisure, health and community centres and operate across a network of organisations (multi-agencies) often representing different sectors of public service provision. Local people's health needs are not necessarily aligned to one sole agency and thus a multi-agency approach to promoting healthy behaviours is advocated for better solutions to community health (Davis and MacDowell 2006). It is typical that allied and/or community health professionals and other partner organisations, possibly outside the health sector (local authority, business, charity, schools etc.) attempt to work collaboratively in the design, delivery and administration of CBOPs; known as an 'intersectoral approach' (Kleij et al. 2015). To establish effective health strategies across the community and partnerships or 'coalitions' between individuals and organisations with a shared interest, work together create a collaborative network to promote, deliver and maintain services (Hawe et al. 1997, Butterfoss 2006). Partnerships between professionals of agencies and leaders can influence long-term health and welfare practices of local people, particularly if the alliances are strong and withstanding (Butterfoss et al. 1993).

At times of austerity and restrictive public service spending in Europe (Karanikolos et al. 2013) and the United Kingdom (Reeves et al. 2013) it would be reasonable to assume that a greater emphasis would place upon social networks and partnership working between public health orientated originations. One major advantage is the sharing of resources (Markwell et al. 2003) particularly spending budgets. Stakeholders interviewed in Middleton et al. (2014) reported that a CBOP demanded a wide range of resources and reported that marketing, hire of buildings/facilities, and purchasing specialist equipment were the main expenses. In this study local authority departments were keen to share resources and keep costs down for the benefit of both parties. Sectors can 'share the wealth' and strong multi-agency networks can potentially share human or technical expertise along with the burden of financing health initiatives (Butterfoss et al. 1993, Butterfoss 2006).

Partnerships can problem solve together providing joint solutions to organisational political pressures regarding public health management (Davis and MacDowell 2006). Such collaborative processes notionally create social capital (Gillies 1998, Muntaner et al. 2000, Morgan and Swann 2004), bonding partners and facilitating the development of norms, values and trust

(Dhillion 2009). The availability of secure networks and resources enabling social connections for community groups should be seen as an important ingredient for developing social capital between partner agencies involved in CBOPs (Holtgrave and Crosby 2006, Moore et al. 2009). Successful multi-agency alliances of the past tackled broad determinants of health in populations together, enabling the advancement of the social capital and subsequently reducing health inequalities in local areas (Gillies 1998). Indeed, mortality rates can be powerfully affected by social capital (Putnam 2000).

Given the importance to partnership working, a primary aim of a CBOP should be to generate local social capital; an effective illustration of communities and organisations involved in facilitating coordination, cooperation and reciprocity (Gillies 1998). For instance, if a network of resources is available for the community to access, it is likely this will increase physical activity and healthy eating practices with encouragement and support. Partnership working has been undervalued despite being of real practical significance to health promotion at community levels (Davis and MacDowell 2006). Relationships should exist in CBOPs for both key delivery purposes and through a coordinated approach to the sharing of goals, development of policies, plans or activities and sustained local action. These are elements of effective collaborative practice (Markwell et al. 2003) and at the same time coalitions should be responsible for strengthening the 'social fabric' in the community (Butterfoss et al. 1993).

Inter-sectorial collaboration can, however, be challenging and researchers (Po'e et al. 2010, Dreisinger, et al. 2012) in this area have suggested that CBOPs would benefit from deepening the network's relationships to facilitate better communication between organisations, integrating services further and enhancing the overall efficiency of delivery practices. It has been argued that the development of networks does not necessarily preclude positive outcomes. Instead, as networks are constituted of relationships between groups and individuals, the development of networks can actually facilitate the production and reproduction of power inequalities (Blackshaw and Long 2005). In addition, it has been noted how power struggles and competing agendas can be apparent within partnerships formed with other organisations and bodies (Frisby et al. 2004; Hayhurst and Frisby 2010; Mackintosh 2011). Moreover, the 'darker side' of partnership working has also been identified in terms of the development of social capital (Numerato and Baglioni 2012; Rowe 2006). For example, partnership dynamics can be solely reliant on how well any potential power struggles are managed (Anderson and Jap 2005; Coulson 2005) as powerful and subordinate groups resist, reproduce and transform policies. At the same time, power dynamics can mean that the domination of one partner over another can see the subordinate partner's views lost (Rowe 2006), or potentially, agencies work to conflicting agendas using different methods of delivery (Evans and Sleap 2013).

Consequentially, CBOP stakeholders have highlighted communication and marketing issues as a real hardship in relation to the effort to create supportive systems, implement partnership work and to avoid replication of efforts (Middleton et al. 2014). The challenge of implementing a CBOP is now well documented; in Australia (Wilson et al. 2009, de Groot et al. 2010, de Silva-Sanigorki et al. 2010), America (Boyle et al. 2009, Po'e et al. 2010, Dreisinger, et al. 2012), Canada (Tucker 2006) and England (Davey et al. 2011, Middleton et al. 2014) stakeholders viewed programmes as taking substantial time and effort to establish and generate impact. The view from a recent systematic review looking at inter-sectorial community approaches outlined that the most influencing factors behind implementation efforts were 'collaboration between community partners,' the 'availability of resources' and 'time available for implementation' (Kleij et al. 2015). A further critical component is thought to be the requirement of strategic leadership, direction and coherent decision making. It is felt that leadership is valuable to the capacity building process, along with established responsibilities for the involved partner organisations (de Groot et al. 2010, Middleton et al. 2014). Given the scale of some CBOPs, it is quite apparent that these initiatives can become unwieldy without significant attention to management and administration and therefore leadership and clear roles for all partner agencies is necessary for successful implementation efforts.

In addition, the extent of community deprivation and social problems (Wilkinson and Pickett 2007) can be a real stumbling block for public health workers tasked with administering CBOPs. Community development work can be complex with layers of inherent difficulty preventing health promotion action (Swinburn et al. 2007). Socio-economic issues for example are known to may influence low levels of engagement in activities which promote healthy behaviours of people with lower socioeconomic status (Pampel et al. 2010). Since the economic crisis and the austerity measures implemented by many European governments; gaps in social, economic and health inequalities are likely to have been exacerbated (Marmort et al. 2012). Indeed, community members felt that the nature of CBOPs activities had little significance to those people in deprived communities under severe financial strain and pressures (Middleton et al. 2014). It is known that challenging dynamic social, cultural and environmental components exist at local community levels (see Economos and Irish-Hauser 2007) and for those administrating CBOPs, careful consideration of the very nature of the community fabric is necessary for understanding the level of likely engagement from community people in a programme.

National reforms in the English health system (abolition of Primary Care Trusts in early 2013) caused local Public Health Directorates (and in essence, public health services including health improvement teams) to move into the local authority organisations (DoH 2010, Pollock and Price 2011). Despite some caution to the reforms (Asthana 2011), this move has produced the opportunity for partnerships between public health workers and local authority staff to solidify and colleagues to work more conjointly or side-by-side. It is likely the move may lead to clearer strategic management of any CBOPs (Middleton et al. 2014). It would also be reasonable to assume that the management of programmes may become more controllable and transparent with the potential for fewer agencies involved. In-turn, collaboration will be strengthened producing productive tracking and monitoring processes involved in implementation and evaluating programmes. Those involved in administration of CBOPs should carefully consider the components in this commentary which highlight the partnership work necessary in the capacity building of CBOPs and building local social capital. Moreover, administrators must pay attention to the potential issues regarding the complexity of the task of creating and implementing effective CBOPs.

References

Allender, S., Nichols, M., Foulkes, C., Reynolds, R., Waters, E., King, L., Gill, T., Armstrong, R. and Swinburn, B. (2011) The development of a network for community-based obesity prevention: the CO-OPS collaboration. *BMC Public Health,* 1, 132-140.

Allender, S., Owen, B., Kuhlberg, J., Lowe, J., Nagorcka-Smith, P., Whelan, J., and Bell, C. (2015) A Community Based Systems Diagram of Obesity Causes. *PloS One,* 10(7), DOI:10.1371/journal.pone.0129683.

Anderson, E., and Jap, S. D. (2005) The dark side of close relationships. *MIT Sloan Management Review*, 46(3), 75-82.

Asthana, S. (2011) Liberating the NHS? A commentary on the Lansley White Paper, "Equity and Excellence." *Social Science and Medicine*, 72(6), 815-820.

Baillie, E., Bjarnholt, C., Gruber, M. and Hughes, R. (2009) A capacity-building conceptual framework for public health nutrition practice. *Public Health Nutrition,* 12, 1031-1038.

Blackshaw, T., and Long, J. (2005) What's the big idea? A critical exploration of the concept of social capital and its incorporation into leisure policy discourse. *Leisure Studies,* 24(3), 239-258.

Boyle, M., Lawrence, S., Schwarte, L., Samuels, S. and McCarthy, W. J. (2009) Health care providers' perceived role in changing environments to promote healthy eating and physical activity: baseline findings from the health care providers participating in the healthy eating, active communities program. *Pediatrics,* 123, S293-S300.

Butterfoss, F. (2006) Building allies coalitions: why formation matters. *Health Promotion Practice*, 7, S23-33.

Butterfoss, F., Goodman, R., Wandersman, A. (1993) Community coalitions for prevention and health promotion. *Health Education Research*, 8, 315-330.

Cecchini, M., Sassi, F., Lauer, J., A. Lee, Y., Guajardo-Barron, V. and Chisholm, D. (2010) Tackling of unhealthy diets, physical inactivity, and obesity: health effects and cost-effectiveness. *Lancet*, 376, 1775-1784.

Coulson, A. (2005) A plague on all your partnerships: theory and practice in regeneration. *International Journal of Public Sector Management,* 18(2), 151-163.

Davey, R., Hurst, G., Smith, G., Grogan, S. and Kurth, J. (2011) The impact and process of a community-led intervention on reducing environmental inequalities related to physical activity and healthy eating - a pilot study. *BMC Public Health,* 11, 697-705.

Davies, M., MacDowall, W. (2006) *Health Promotion Theory: Understanding Public Health.* Maidenhead: Open University Press.

de Groot, F., Robertson, N., Swinburn, B. and Silva-Sanigorski, A. (2010) Increasing community capacity to prevent childhood obesity: challenges, lessons learned and results from the Romp and Chomp intervention. *BMC Public Health,* 10, 522-530.

de Silva-Sanigorski, A. M., Bolton, K., Haby, M., Kremer, P., Gibbs, L., Waters, E. and Swinburn, B. (2010) Scaling up community-based obesity prevention in Australia: Background and evaluation design of the Health Promoting Communities: Being Active Eating Well initiative. *BMC Public Health,* 10, 65-72.

DeMattia, L. and Denney, S. (2008) Childhood Obesity Prevention: Successful Community-Based Efforts. *The ANNALS of the American Academy of Political and Social Science*, 615, 83-99.

Department of Communities and Local Government (2011) *English Indices of Deprivation 2010.* London: HMSO. Available at: https://www.gov.uk/government/statistics/english-indices-of-deprivation-2010 (Accessed 3rd Sept 2015).

Department of Health (2010) *The White Paper. Equity and excellence: liberating the NHS.* London: Department of Health. Available at: https://www.gov.uk/government/uploads/system/uploads/attachment_data/file/213823/dh_117794.pdf (Accessed 3rd Sept 2015).

Dhillon, J. (2009) The role of social capital in sustaining partnership. *British Educational Research Journal*, 35, 687-704.

Dreisinger, M., Boland, E., Filler, C., Baker, E., Hessel, A. and Brownson, R. (2012) Contextual factors influencing readiness for dissemination of obesity prevention programs and policies. *Health Education Research,* 27 (2), 292-306.

Economos, C. and Irish-Hauser, S. (2007) Community interventions: a brief overview and their application to the obesity epidemic. *The Journal of Law, Medicine and Ethics*, 35, 131–137.

Evans, A. B., and Sleap, M. (2013) " Swim for Health": program evaluation of a multi-agency aquatic activity intervention in the United Kingdom. *International Journal of Aquatic Research and Education*, 7(1), 24-38.

Frisby, W., Thibault, L., and Kikulis, L. (2004). The organizational dynamics of under-managed partnerships in leisure service departments. *Leisure Studies,* 23(2), 109-126.

Gillies, P. (1998) Effectiveness of alliances and partnerships for health promotion. *Health Promotion International,* 13, 99-119.

Gortmaker, S. L., Swinburn, B., Levy, D., Carter, R., Mabry, P., Finegood, D., Huang, T, Marsh, T. and Moodie, M. (2011) Changing the future of obesity: science, policy, and action. *Lancet*, 378, 838-847.

Hawe, P., Noort, M., King, L., and Jordens, C. (1997) Multiplying health gains: the critical role of capacity-building in health promotion programs. *Health Policy*, 39, 29-42.

Hayhurst, L. M., and Frisby, W. (2010). Inevitable tensions: Swiss and Canadian sport for development NGO perspectives on partnerships with high performance sport. *European Sport Management Quarterly,* 10(1), 75-96.

Holtgrave, D.R., Crosby, R. (2006) Is social capital a protective factor against obesity and diabetes? Findings from an exploratory study. *Annals of Epidemiology,* 16, 406–408.

Karanikolos, M., Mladovsky, P., Cylus, J., Thomson, S., Basu, S., Stuckler, D., Mackenbach, J and McKee, M. (2013) Financial crisis, austerity, and health in Europe. *The Lancet*, 381(9874), 1323-1331.

King, L., Gill, T., Allender, S. and Swinburn, B. (2011) Best practice principles for community-based prevention: development, content and application. *Obesity Reviews,* 12, 329-338.

Kumanyika, S., Obarzanek, E., Stettler, N., Bell, R., Field, A., Fortmann, S., Franklin, B., Gillman, M., Lewis, C., Poston, W., Stevens, J. and Hong, Y. (2008) Population-based prevention of obesity: the need for comprehensive promotion of healthful eating, physical activity, and energy balance: a scientific statement from American Heart Association Council on Epidemiology and Prevention, Interdisciplinary Committee for Prevention. *Circulation,* 118, 428-464.

Liberato, S., Brimblecombe, J., Ritchie, J., Ferguson, M. and Coveney, J. (2011) Measuring capacity building in communities: a review of the literature. *BMC Public Health,* 11, 850-860.

Mackintosh, C. (2011) An analysis of County Sports Partnerships in England: the fragility, challenges and complexity of partnership working in sports development. *International Journal of Sport Policy and Politics*, 3(1), 45-64.

Markwell, S., Watson, J., Speller, V., Platt, S., Younger, T. (2003) *The Working Partnership - Book 1*, London: Health Development Agency.

Marmot, M., Allen, J., Bell, R., Bloomer, E., and Goldblatt, P. (2012) WHO European review of social determinants of health and the health divide. *The Lancet*, 380, 1011-1029.

Moore, S., Daniel, M., Paquet, C., Dubé, L., Gauvin, L. (2009) Association of individual network social capital with abdominal adiposity, overweight and obesity. *Journal of Public Health*, 31, 175-183.

Morgan, A. and Swann, C. (2004) *Social capital for health issues of definition, measurement and links to health*. London: Health Development Agency.

Muntaner, C. and Lynch, J., Smith, G. (2000) Social capital and the third way in public health. *Critical Public Health,* 10, 107-124.

Naidoo, J. and Willis, J. (2009) *Foundations for Health Promotion*, 3rd ed. London: Bailliere Tindall.

Numerato, D., and Baglioni, S. (2012) The dark side of social capital: An ethnography of sport governance. *International Review for the Sociology of Sport*, 47(5), 594-611.

Pampel, F. C., Krueger, P. M., and Denney, J. T. (2010). Socioeconomic disparities in health behaviors. *Annual Review of Sociology*, 36, 349-370.

Po'e, E., Gesell, S., Lynne Caples, T., Escarfuller, J. and Barkin, S. (2010) Pediatic obesity community programs: barriers and facilitators toward sustainability. *Journal of Community Health*, 35, 348-354.

Pollock, A. M., and Price, D. (2011). How the secretary of state for health proposes to abolish the NHS in England. *British Medical Journal*, 342, 800-803.

Putnam, R. (2000). *Bowling Alone: The Collapse and Revival of American Community*. New York, US: Simon and Schuster.

Reeves, A., Basu, S., McKee, M., Marmot, M., and Stuckler, D. (2013). Austere or not? UK coalition government budgets and health inequalities. *Journal of the Royal Society of Medicine,* 106(11), 432-436.

Rowe, M. (2006). Abusive partnerships: New forms of governance, new forms of abuse? *International Journal of Sociology and Social Policy,* 26(5-6) 207-219.

Simmons, A., Mavoa, H., Bell, A. (2009) Creating community action plans for obesity prevention using the ANGELO (Analysis Grid for Elements Linked to Obesity) Framework. *Health Promotion International,* 24, 311-324.

Swinburn, B., Bell, C., King, L., Magarey, A., O'Brien, K., Waters, E. (2007) Obesity prevention programs demand high-quality evaluations. *Australian and New Zealand Journal of Public Health*, 31, 305-307.

Swinburn, B., Sacks, G., Hall, K., McPherson, K., Finegood, D., Moodie, M. and Gortmaker, S. (2011) The global obesity pandemic: shaped by global drivers and local environments. *Lancet*, 378, 804-14.

Tucker, P., Irwin, J., Sangster Bouck, L., He, M. and Pollett, G. (2006) Preventing paediatric obesity; recommendations from a community-based qualitative investigation. *Obesity Reviews*, 7, 251-260.

Wang, C., McPherson, K., Marsh, T., Gortmaker, S. and Brown, M. (2011) Health and economic burden of the projected obesity trends in the USA and the UK. *Lancet*, 378, 815-25.

Wilkinson, R.G., Pickett, K.E. (2007) The problems of relative deprivation: why some societies do better than others. *Social Science and Medicine*, 65, 1965-1978.

Wilson, A., Magarey, A., Dollman, J., Jones, M., Mastersson, N. (2009) The challenges of quantitative evaluation of a multi-setting, multi-strategy community-based childhood obesity prevention programme: lessons learnt from the eat well be active Community Programs in South Australia. *Public Health Nutrition,* 13, 1262-1270.

World Health Organisation (2004) *Obesity: Preventing and Managing the Global Epidemic: Report of a WHO Consultation*. Technical Report Series no.894. Geneva, Switzerland: WHO. Available at: http://www.who.int/nutrition/publications/obesity/WHO_TRS_894/en/ (Accessed 3rd Sept 2015).

World Health Organization. (2012). *Population-based approaches to childhood obesity prevention.* Geneva, Switzerland: WHO. Available at: http://www.who.int/dietphysicalactivity/childhood/WHO_new_childhood obesity_PREVENTION_27nov_HR_PRINT_OK.pdf (Accessed 3rd Sept 2015).

In: Capacity Building
Editor: Diane Brown
ISBN: 978-1-63483-995-2

Chapter 3

BUILDING CAPACITY TOWARDS HIV PREVENTION IN A LATINO MIGRANT WORKER COMMUNITY IN SOUTH FLORIDA

Jesús Sánchez*[*]*, PhD
Department of Sociobehavioral and Administrative Pharmacy,
College of Pharmacy, Nova Southeastern University,
Fort Lauderdale, FL, US

ABSTRACT

Despite an growing array of efficacious interventions tailored to immigrant and migrant populations in the US, there are mounting challenges in developing strategies that prevent and control HIV and other sexually transmitted infections (STIs), and that can be sustained and scaled to meet the needs of those most vulnerable to their impact. Community-based participatory research (CBPR) has received increasing recognition as a public health paradigm that combines epidemiology and behavioral science in order to understand how multiple determinants interact to influence health in a particular community. CBPR requires an equitable partnership between researchers and those directly affected by

---

[*] Correspondence: Professor Jesús Sánchez, Ph.D. Associate Professor, Department of Sociobehavioral and Administrative Pharmacy, College of Pharmacy, Nova Southeastern University, 3200 South University Drive, Fort Lauderdale, FL 33328-2018. E-mail: js2769@nova.edu

and knowledgeable of the local circumstances that impact health in a given community. Tangible, lasting health benefits require a balance of rigorous research that respectfully, productively, and equally involves community partners.

In this chapter, we offer our reflections on a CBPR project in partnership with the Latino migrant worker community in South Florida. We first discussed how we forged a partnership (known in the community as Project Salud) between researchers and community members. Next, we present the results and evaluate the efficacy of a community-based intervention to reduce risk behaviors and enhance mediators of HIV-preventative behaviors. Finally, we attempt to discuss some of the challenges inherent in CBPR and reflect on the question, "is CBPR a good fit?" We aim for our analysis to contribute a unique perspective to the rich, ongoing discussion about developing community capacity as a means to promote health, ameliorate health disparities, and promote justice in marginalized, vulnerable communities.

Introduction

Latinos in the United States continue to be impacted by the HIV/AIDS epidemic, having higher rates of both new HIV infections and people living with HIV disease than their white counterparts [1-4]. More specifically, the Latino migrant and immigrant populations in the US have been particularly affected. Understanding and addressing the causes of HIV related health disparities among Latinos in the U.S. is increasingly relevant as the magnitude of immigrant and migrant populations from Central and South America and the Caribbean continue to grow [5-6].

Research has specifically linked migration to increased HIV incidence and vulnerability in a variety of contexts and places. A greater risk for poor health and limited access to health services, low socioeconomic status, low levels of formal education, and marginalization are among the main reasons why Latino migrant workers (LMWs) are particularly vulnerable to HIV infection [6-7]. The few available studies on HIV transmission and prevention specifically conducted among Latino migrant workers highlight the role played by many complex and interrelated factors. These include social norms, health-related beliefs, attitudes and behaviors related to sex and drug use, and social and environmental factors such as housing and employment [8-12]. LMWs bring with them an assortment of beliefs, attitudes, and practices that vary from country to country of origin and that—when put into practice in their new communities—often result in a sense of cultural shock, stress, and alienation that may impact health-risk behaviors, in general, and HIV related risk behaviors in particular. The development of effective HIV prevention interventions for the Latino migrant worker community requires that we address the cultural and societal issues that put LMWs at risk as well as focus on the cultural strengths that might assist members of this community to stay safe.

Despite a dire need for the development, implementation, and evaluation of HIV prevention interventions designed to reduce the risk of infection among Latinos lags behind prevention efforts targeting other communities [13]. This public health gap is particularly apparent when considering the sparse attention received by Latino migrant workers in the United States despite their high risk for HIV infection. Research indicates that most Latino migrant workers (LMWs) become infected while in the U.S., underlining the importance of enhancing both HIV prevention and treatment efforts [14].

While existing studies have made a critical contribution to advance our understanding of the Latino migrant worker population in the US and highlight numerous potential differences between this and other populations, their HIV prevention interventions have demonstrated only limited effectiveness [15-17] and documented a critical need for tailoring effective HIV prevention interventions for the Latino migrant worker population. These adaptations, however, cannot be limited to the cultural translation of existing interventions based on cultural generalizations or preconceptions associated with Latinos [18-19]. A pervasive limitation of many of these cultural translations involves the use of the umbrella category "Latino" (or "Hispanic") which presents an obfuscated description that pretends to capture the characteristics of a large group of national and ethnic populations. Another important limitation is the imposition of the term "Latino" on different subgroups with different characteristics, backgrounds, and migration experiences without asking members of these groups for their opinion. These limitations contribute to the traditional mistrust among LMWs of conventional research which they view as paternalistic, misguided, and irrelevant to their needs. As a result, conventional prevention strategies are likely to fail to adequately help Latino migrant workers to adopt and maintain HIV risk reduction behaviors in a constantly shifting personal and social environment [20-22]. Culturally adapted interventions must prompt community engagement and participation at every phase of the program if they do not want to remain culturally blind. Latino migrant workers are most likely to benefit from HIV prevention efforts when these efforts are supported at the community level, sustained over time, and the overall needs of the community are addressed [23-25].

Community based participatory research (CBPR) has emerged as a research paradigm that addresses the limitations of conventional research models and offers a "collaborative approach to research that equitably involves all partners in the research process and recognizes the unique strengths that each brings. The ultimate goal is to promote social change to improve community health and reduce health disparities" [26]. Advantages of CBPR include that it is a participatory and cooperative approach, requires equitable power and mutual ownership, is framed in a co-learning experience, and seeks the balance between research and action. Furthermore, it is an empowering process that involves capacity building among all partners involved.

Building capacity to improve health involves the development of sustainable skills, resources, and organizational structures in the affected community. For empowerment efforts to be equitable, effective, and sustainable, all stakeholders must be ready for collaboration and leadership. Thus, building capacity also includes fostering shared knowledge, leadership skills, and an ability to represent the interests of one's constituents. Because capacity building is deeply rooted in the social, political, and economic environment, it cannot be conducted without an understanding of the specific environment in which it will take place [27]. When carried out with context in mind, capacity building is an integral part of community engagement efforts, necessary for challenging power imbalances and effectively addressing problems.

In this chapter, we offer our reflections on a CBPR project in partnership with the Latino migrant worker community in South Florida. We first discussed how we forged a partnership (known in the community as Project Salud) between researchers and community members. Next, we present the results and evaluate the efficacy of a community-based intervention to reduce risk behaviors and enhance mediators of HIV-preventative behaviors. Finally, we attempt to discuss some of the challenges inherent in CBPR and reflect on the question, "is CBPR a good fit?" We aim for our analysis to contribute a unique perspective to the rich, ongoing discussion about developing community capacity as a means to promote health, ameliorate health disparities, and promote justice in marginalized, vulnerable communities.

Developing Project Salud

Project Salud--officially entitled "HIV Risk Reduction among High Risk Latino Migrant Workers in South Florida"--was a 4-year major study funded by the National Institute on Minority Health and Health Disparities (NIMHD). The main objective of Project Salud was to assess the differential effectiveness of an Adapted Stage-Enhanced Motivational Interviewing (A-SEMI) compared to a Health Promotion Comparison (HPC) condition for producing long-term reductions in HIV risk and increased health behaviors among LMWs. Project Salud was conceived as a CBPR project with the goal of engaging the Latino migrant worker community in the Homestead/Florida City area in the implementation of an HIV prevention intervention. By framing Project Salud within the CBPR approach, this study responded to the NIH priority on establishing equitable partnerships between community members and researchers with the final goal of increasing community participation in the research process, improving community health, and reducing HIV-related health disparities.

As described in this paper, the A-SEMI intervention was culturally adapted in collaboration with the LMW community. At the early stages of Project Salud, we set off a plan to address the issue of cultural adaptation while reinforcing trust in the community and creating community capacity as a key building block in the development of our partnership with the Latino migrant worker community. We initiated a dialogue with key community partners and community members with the goal of identifying what type of strategies would be adequate to address the issue of HIV prevention among Latino migrant workers. The ultimate goal of this dialogue was to juxtapose the views of both the community and the researchers. Based on this exchange of ideas and using other researchers' experiences as a learning framework [28-30], we decided that focus group methodology was the appropriate approach. Researchers who work with migrant populations have reported on the complexities of working with these populations and how a unique sensitivity is required to understand how particular phenomena are experienced and expressed [31]. Focus groups provide several advantages over the conventional methods in instrument development. First, focus groups are useful for developing insights into the perceptions and points of view of persons who have some common characteristics related to the research topic and for appreciating the variation in people's experiences [32]. The resulting intervention is more likely to be grounded in the experiences of the population under study. Generating knowledge from focus groups can provide reasonable assurance that the instrument is culturally anchored. Second, focus groups inform researchers about the language and terminology that particular groups of people use regarding the construct under study [32]. By preserving the terminology from the focus group, items included in the intervention may reflect the language of the population of interest. Third, the focus group's social nature often stimulates stories and insights that would be missed otherwise [33].

Focus groups were conducted at the early stages of Project Salud when both the project and the researchers involved in it were still unknown to many community members. We undertook a series of preparatory activities prior to conducting the focus groups to better inform the Latino migrant worker community in Homestead about who we were, the goals of the project, and our desire to establish a true partnership with the community. As part of these preparatory steps, we conducted several town hall meetings at venues such as churches, street markets, a community center, and the offices of the Farmworker Association of Florida in the Homestead/Florida City area. We expanded our partnership with professionals in health and social services, advocates, religious leaders, AIDS educators and, more importantly, nursery and agricultural workers. As our partnership grew larger and stronger, Project Salud started being recognized in the community.

Another positive outcome of our increasing presence and recognition in the community resulted in the implementation of strategies that increased recruitment rates and representativeness. Community members' concerns about becoming involved in a focus group began to dissipate during town hall meetings and the different activities conducted at the early stages of the project. The support of community partners was crucial at a time when the current anti-immigration climate and policies in the U.S. have negatively impacted the lives of migrant workers. We addressed this issue by validating such concerns and extensively reviewing the standards of confidentiality and the rights of each participant (i.e., right to withdraw from the study at any time, right to refuse to answer questions). We also adopted community members' suggestions regarding the locations where we could meet and conduct the focus groups. The suggested sites--unlike some of the locations we had originally preselected--were considered by the community as safer and less likely to be raided by immigration authorities.

To be selected for the focus groups, participants had to (a) be 18 years old or older; (b) be a first generation immigrant; (c) be a member of the Latino migrant worker community in the Homestead area; and (d) express an interest to participate in the focus group interview.

A total of eight focus groups were conducted with a range of 6 to 12 participants per focus group. A maximum number of 12 participants per group was established in order to better facilitate group discussions. Each focus group interview lasted between 120 and 180 minutes and was held in the evening and/or weekend. All focus groups started with a dinner, an overview of Project Salud, completion of a consent form, and brief demographic questionnaire. Each participant received a $40 stipend for their participation. Participants were required by IRB policy to complete a form documenting their receipt of the participant payment; however, no personal identifiers were requested.

Eighty-three members of the Latino migrant worker community participated in the focus groups. Although it was planned in the original research protocol to organize focus groups according to a set of criteria (i.e., gender, nationality, age), the design was modified in response to the contextual challenges associated with recruitment. In particular, participants were encouraged to join whichever focus group was possible for them to attend.

Focus groups were consistent in their delivery and draw upon the same protocol guidelines. Each session was facilitated by a project member with experience in focus group facilitation while another project member was present at each session as a note-taker. Focus groups were conducted in Spanish and the discussions were audio recorded and then transcribed for purposes of data analysis. Prior to conducting the focus groups, we hired two members from the LMW community to be trained on the project, assist with the development of the focus group protocol, and support focus group sessions.

Project Salud members introduced themselves and provided a five to ten minute overview of the project. Project members made this presentation highly interactive as a means to warm up the focus group participants. For instance, they included a trivia or guessing game as part of the presentation. Group members introduced themselves and were invited to briefly express an opinion on the impact of the HIV/AIDS epidemic on their community. This initial discussion provided a context for the group from which to proceed. Participants were told that focus groups were being held in order to learn from the Latino migrant worker community about their knowledge, behaviors, and attitudes towards the HIV/AIDS epidemic. They were also inquired about their interest in participating in a study that would utilize the information learned from the focus groups to determine how the different intervention components should be adapted and implemented in order to increase community members' motivation to participate in this initiative and establish a sustainable strategy for implementing the adapted intervention in the community.

Project Salud members explained that the research team sought to offer an existing evidence-based HIV prevention intervention to the LMW community that had proven beneficial to other communities. Therefore, the focus group sessions were a key step toward clarifying how relevant LMWs find the specific core components (i.e., skills) covered in the original intervention, exploring if the intervention was responsive to their life experiences and cultural background, and making the necessary cultural adaptations. The ensuing discussion followed the protocol guidelines tailored to explore and discuss the core components of the evidence-based intervention.

Using focus groups proved to be a challenging but successful experience that provided many insights into culturally shaping the A-SEMI intervention. Talking about HIV-related behaviors, attitudes, and beliefs in a group setting can be extremely difficult for Latino men and women who view topics such as sexual behaviors as very personal. Because of this, we found that some participants would talk about these issues as if they were happening to a friend or relative. On the other hand, we also concluded that—although less private—the use of oral and group-centered strategies were more reflective of the dominant learning styles, orientations, values and educational levels of participants. As a result, although an interventionist would typically encourage participants to talk about their own experiences and opinions, we agreed that when working with the LMW community, we needed to be aware that—in some instances—one strategy to cope with the discomfort of talking about personal issues is to frame it as the experience of someone else.

The focus groups also revealed the need for a more dynamic understanding of the cultural milieu that characterizes Latino migrant worker communities. An example of how sweeping assertions about Latino culture fail to capture the shifting cultural dynamics of this community is reflected in the impact of changing gender roles on sexual relations. Traditional gender roles are often associated with Latino culture. *Machismo* and *marianismo* are presented as playing a crucial role in shaping sexual communication and relations between Latino men and women [34]. Because of the apparent power imbalance that characterizes these relationships, some scholars suggest that theories that emphasize sexual division of labor and power may be an appropriate intervention framework. However, our focus groups revealed that—although often times this power imbalance may have characterized participants' sexual relations in their countries of origin—as LMWs spend more time away from their countries of origin, they begin to reconsider those gender role expectations. This trend was particularly salient among the women who participated in the focus groups. Having to endure the same harsh working and housing conditions as their male counterparts, Latina migrant workers question the traditional idea of the submissive Latina who centers her life on her family and is generally obedient to the men in her life. As a result, sexual culture in the LMW community can be characterized as the coexistence of traditional and modern values. In light of this finding, it was crucial to culturally adapt the A-SEMI intervention to reflect the coexisting cultural expectations and rules of sexual interaction among LMWs.

Another salient value associated with traditional Latino culture is *familismo*, which places the multigenerational extended family at the core of the culture. *Familismo* promotes closeness and interconnectedness among extended family members and provides a sense of responsibility to care for all members of the family [34]. Most of the participants in the focus groups had few or no relatives living with them in the U.S. Many of the male participants indicated that they came to the U.S. by themselves and would not risk bringing their families over because of the risks associated with getting smuggled into the U.S. Other participants indicated that their spouses or significant others had been deported back to their countries of origin and, in most cases, were trying to cross the border again. As a result, the positive impact provided by *familismo* in terms of social support, knowledge, and material resources is lacking in the LMW community. In its absence, participants stressed the importance of developing a sense of community. Participants highlighted the importance of facilitating learning experiences by promoting a sense of community among those who would participate in the intervention. Specifically, rather than limiting group interventions to didactic sessions focused exclusively on disseminating knowledge and teaching skills, participants affirmed that interventions should also promote group cohesion and supportive relationships among intervention participants. Many participants in the focus groups commented on how valuable the focus group session was to them, as well as their desire to extend the same type of dynamic into the intervention. Participants expressed that the intervention groups should constitute a resource for empowering participants. Consequently, the A-SEMI intervention was culturally adapted to enhance empowerment as a multilayered process beyond the cultural domains directly related to HIV prevention (i.e., sexual relations).

Conducting Project Salud

A network-based sample of 278 Latino migrant workers was recruited from November 2008 to December 2010 from migrant communities in the Homestead area in Miami-Dade County, Florida. Homestead is part of a predominantly rural area in the South of Miami-Dade County, Florida. Official census data indicate that most of the population in Homestead (51.8%) is Hispanic/Latino, more than one-third (36%) is foreign born, and a majority (57.3%) speaks a language other than English at home [35]. Agriculture and nursery constitute an important business in the Homestead area allowing for access to seasonal farm work. Homestead's Latino migrant worker population is composed primarily of recently arrived, young, single or married men that are in the United States alone. They live in small crowded apartments with family or friends. Most are Mexican and Central American arriving in this area with little or no English language skills and very limited resources.

After screening for eligibility, participants were administered a structured baseline questionnaire using A-CASI that included basic socio-demographic information, alcohol and other drug use history, sexual behaviors, acculturation, and behavioral intentionality. Study participants were then randomly assigned to the A-SEMI and HPC intervention groups.

The design of the A-SEMI intervention was guided by the theoretical foundations of social cognitive theory [36] enhanced with peer education and motivational enhancing therapy with the objective of producing a stronger, more sustained HIV risk reduction effect among LMWs. Two trained CHWs delivered A-SEMI in Spanish during four 2.5-hour interactive group sessions that took place at the FWAF office in Homestead, FL on two consecutive weekends. Based on their schedule, group participants decided whether they wanted to have two sessions—one in the morning and one in the afternoon—on the same day (i.e., Sunday) or on different days (i.e., one session on Saturday and another session on Sunday). On average, each group was composed of six participants. Session 1 of A-SEMI focused on developing group cohesion and addressing HIV education. Session 2 was devoted to motivational enhancement and goal setting. Study subjects were helped in developing a specific and relevant personal risk-reduction plan that could be realistically accomplished with a sense of mastery and success. Session 3 focused on increasing commitment to and empowerment for safer sex. Session 4 focused on identifying high-risk situations and negotiation skills through problem solving, assertiveness, and communication.

A Peer Counseling Intervention Component (PCIC) was integrated into the A-SEMI. PCIC has been employed in a number of effective HIV intervention studies [37-41]. One of the strongest theoretical factors to a PCIC approach involves peer credibility. Community members—especially in isolated and hard to reach social environments—identify their peers as reliable and preferred sources of information on sexuality-related topics, including sexually transmitted infections and HIV. As a result, peers are more effective educators and yield higher levels of commitment.

Motivational Enhancing Therapy (MET) has been integrated into effective interventions for reducing substance abuse and HIV risk behaviors [42, 43]. Existing studies revealed that in many instances participants could demonstrate adequate post-intervention skills and knowledge associated with reducing risk, but lacked the motivation to actually do so. This evidence prompted us to incorporate MET strategies into A-SEMI. One added MET component is the provision of normative feedback. Based on the baseline assessment, normative feedback will be offered to assist A-SEMI participants in identifying reasons for changing HIV attitudes and risk behavior, and in eliciting self-motivating statements. This addition was based on Kalichman's et al. [44] adaptation for group administration of the MET normative feedback technique for HIV prevention. The influence of MET is also reflected in A-SEMI, which throughout places great emphasis on actively engaging participants in developing their own risk-reduction strategies and hierarchies of safety, rather than prescribing specific strategies as in a more traditional cognitive behavioral interventions. When participants actively choose and develop risk reduction strategies, this tends to increase personal involvement and the motivation to change [43].

For instance, Session 2 began with a brief review of Session 1 during which CHWs had initiated a discussion about ways to prevent HIV infection, including the use of condoms. Groups members were provided with feedback that included their responses to the condom attitude measure collected at baseline. Condom attitudes were discussed via group activities which allowed participants to sort those attitudes into pros and cons of condom use. CHWs utilized the negative aspects of condom use as examples for the problem-solving skills addressed during session 4.

The Health Promotion Condition (HPC) served as the comparison condition and target specific health issues of special relevance to LMWs such as general health strategies such as hygiene and living in crowded conditions, first aid, and skin problems. A-SEMI and HPC were structurally equivalent in administration, time, and format. They also were designed to be of a similar level of interest. Both interventions were guided by a written manual and held at the same community setting with refreshments/snacks, and with identical compensation for participation. Moreover, equal quality control provisions were used, particularly regarding the need to verify that both interventions were delivered as designed (intervention fidelity), which was stressed during training and at the beginning of each session. All intervention sessions were digitally recorded by a staff member attending the sessions. A structured coding system was created and used to determine fidelity based on the digital recordings. The staff member also took notes during the sessions that were utilized to ensure fidelity. Recordings and notes were reviewed by the project staff and discuss during biweekly meetings to ensure fidelity and provide feedback to project staff.

Assessments were conducted at baseline and at 3- and 9-month intervention follow-ups. Data were collected via an audio computer assisted self-interview (ACASI) with the purpose of enhancing confidentiality among participants as well as increasing comprehension among participants with low literacy. A project staff member was always available during data collection to assist participants with any questions and/or technical difficulties. Each assessment was conducted in Spanish and took approximately 90 minutes. A project staff member secured the interviews data as soon as participants had finished the assessment. Following the baseline assessment, participants were randomly assigned to the A-SEMI or HPC interventions using a computer generated randomization table. Following each assessment and intervention session, participants received a monetary incentive as approved by the Institutional Review Board. Analyses were performed using an intent-to-treat protocol in which participants were analyzed in their original assigned study conditions irrespective of the number of sessions attended [45].

Study findings [46] indicate that A-SEMI participants were more likely to engage in safe sexual behaviors compared to HPC participants. Over the entire 9-month period, promising A-SEMI intervention effects were observed for consistent condom use over the last 90 and 30 days prior to assessment. Similarly, positive intervention effects were observed for never having used condoms over the last 90 and 30 days prior to assessment, and using a condom at their last sexual encounter. We also observed favorable changes in hypothesized psychosocial factors for HIV risk reduction over the 9-month follow-up period [46].

Lessons Learned: Capacity Building and Sustainability

Project Salud has been shown to help with HIV prevention efforts in the Latino migrant worker community in South Florida. However, implementation challenges in conducting our study were manifold and deserve to be noted not only for the sake of advancing our partnership with the LMW community but also in terms of sharing our experience with researchers aiming to engage in CBPR. In addition to conducting the type of formative and summative evaluations normally associated with traditional research, we also conducted additional participatory and empowerment research more closely associated with CBPR. Our evaluation revealed the need to address two key, closely linked core components of the CBPR paradigm: capacity building and sustainability. Consolidating and sustaining the knowledge, resources, skills, and values necessary to support CBPR efforts requires time and effort commitments broader than those supported by traditional research and its funding mechanisms. For example, when resources are limited and time is constrained, it is difficult for partners to share critical self-reflection on the ongoing CBPR process in order to make changes as research is being conducted. Another relevant challenge reflects how community members and stakeholders not directly engaged with the project are often unaware of our accomplishments and the benefits of using a CBPR approach. Hence, if the value of CBPR is not fully understood, it is difficult to sustain this capacity building component of a partnership.

Additional funding—via an Administrative Supplement award—by NIMHD provided us with the opportunity to address the issue of capacity building and sustainability in the Latino migrant worker community. This new project is a CBPR-based research education program with the goals of 1) building the knowledge and skills needed at the community level to develop and sustain an effective CBPR partnership; and 2) creating a permanent research facility in the community.

At the early stages, we set off a plan to address the issue of reinforcing trust in the community while creating community capacity as a key building block in the development of our partnership with the Latino migrant worker community. We initiated a dialogue with a broader range of community partners and community members with the goal of identifying what type of knowledge, skills, resources and community values would be necessary to address the issue of HIV prevention among Latino migrant workers and long-term sustainability of these prevention efforts. The ultimate goal of this dialogue was to juxtapose the views of both the community and the researchers.

Based on this exchange of ideas and using other researchers' experiences as a learning framework [26, 47-49], we developed the Latino Migrant Worker HIV Prevention Program (LMW-HIVP). LMW-HIVP is a CBPR-based community health worker education program with the goal of building the knowledge and skills needed at the community level to develop and sustain an effective CBPR partnership to support HIV/AIDS research and prevention in the Latino migrant community.

The LMW-HIVP had three main objectives. The first objective was to develop the LMW-HIVP training curriculum and create a training manual and website based on it. The second objective was to implement the training curriculum to educate community members as community health workers (CHWs) and incorporate them into Project Salud's HIV prevention efforts. The training curriculum included various fundamental aspects of HIV research and prevention including community outreach and education, data collection, and findings dissemination. The third and final objective was to provide the community with a permanent research facility.

Creating the Curriculum

Our first priority was to create a training curriculum that would provide the Latino migrant community with the knowledge and skills to address the issue of HIV research and prevention in their community from a CBPR standpoint. Qualitative methods were utilized to gain an understanding of the sociocultural values, beliefs, and practices in the area of HIV/AIDS of Latino migrant workers working and residing in the Homestead/Florida City area. Ethnographic methods used during the curriculum development phase included participant observations, focus groups, and one-on-one, in-depth, semi-structured interviews. Project Salud staff spent 14 months in the field attending numerous meetings and community events during which the curriculum was developed.

The curriculum included six units: CBPR Principles, Research Ethics, HIV/AIDS and its impact on the Latino community in the U.S., Oral Health, Quantitative Methodology, and Qualitative Methodology. Each unit contained learning objectives, in-depth content information about the topic(s) being presented, examples and interactive exercises that are designed to trigger discussion and to help better understand the concepts being presented, and suggested references and resources. The curriculum was built upon a combination of approaches to teaching and learning and customized to the specific needs of the community. It was also developed to build on and reflect existing community strengths and assets.

Implementation of Training Curriculum

Prior to implementing the training curriculum, we hired two members from the community to be trained on the training curriculum, assist with the development of the training manual, and support training efforts at the community level.

An empowerment model of education was utilized for the delivery of the training program. This model, based on the works of Paulo Freire [50], uses a learning cycle of listening-dialogue-action. The listening phase involves systematic listening of community concerns. The dialogue phase involves a problem-posing method to enable participants in the analysis of their problems including underlying causes. Finally, during the action phase, the facilitator uses structured dialogue within a participatory interactive model for education to help participants identify and reflect on the actions needed to address identified problems individually and socially within the community [51-53].

The implementation of the training curriculum consisted of a workshop that included seven 1-day training sessions. The entire workshop took place over the course of two weeks and training participants received a monetary compensation at the end of session seven. The first six sessions of the training workshop were devoted to each of the six units on the curriculum while session seven was a wrap-up session. Although community participants were welcome to offer their feedback throughout the entire 7-day workshop, we conducted a formal evaluation at the end of session seven. We used participants' comments and the formal evaluation to update and improve the training manual so each new cohort of community participants would benefit from these improvements. Forty-six community members--26 females and 20 males--were trained in cohorts of four to six participants.

The success of a CHW program depends in part on recruiting and training individuals with broad social networks who have the time and desire to pass on their knowledge and skills to other members of the community. Our CHW program presented additional challenges since HIV and related risk behaviors—particularly, sex behaviors—are not typically discussed in the Latino culture33. We selected training participants based on the following eligibility criteria: 1) Latino migrant worker; 2) literate; 3) aged 18 and older; 4) open-minded about discussing HIV and related risk behaviors; and 5) living and residing in the Homestead/Florida City area for, at least, 4 months of the year.

Project Salud staff viewed retention in the LMW-HIVP as not merely completion of the program, but as active participation in all parts of the program. Therefore, the program addressed issues of access on multiple levels including 1) a relevant and accessible curriculum; 2) teaching methods that fit with cultural norms; 3) making transportation and childcare available to training participants; and 4) providing meals, snacks, and beverages at different points during the training sessions.

Creation of a Permanent Research Facility

The third objective of the LMW-HIVP was to provide the community with a permanent research facility that would support the community efforts to promote health and prevent HIV infection over time. In a combined effort between Project Salud and one of its main community partners, the Farmworker Association of Florida (FWAF), we have created a permanent research environment through the creation of a research facility at the offices of the Farmworker Association of Florida in Homestead. This office has been furnished with brand new computer equipment, printers, software, office supplies and—in general—everything that is needed for the day-to-day operation of a research facility, including technical assistance by Project Salud staff. This new research facility is currently housing ongoing research and prevention efforts and serves as a hub for the array of activities being conducted under Project Salud as well as other activities in which the LMW community is interested.

CONCLUSION

Challenges to conducting CBPR are well documented and may discourage researchers and community members from engaging in this type of research [54-56]. Project Salud sought to engage a group of researchers and members/stakeholders in the Latino migrant community in South Florida with the goal of establishing a partnership based on CBPR principles to address HIV prevention. One of the most critical challenges we faced consisted in finding ways in which these prevention efforts could be enhanced and sustained over time. We realized that it was not viable to establish and sustain a true collaborative, equitable research partnership with the Latino migrant worker community unless we could generate capacity building opportunities that could provide members of the community with the necessary knowledge, resources, and skills to enhance and maintain HIV prevention efforts.

In response to this assessment, Project Salud has been genuinely invested in building community capacity by developing and implementing a CHW education training program—LMW-HIVP—and creating a permanent research environment in the community. The training program gave community members an opportunity to acquire knowledge and skills on how to conduct research that were very scarce in the community. The training program was also increasing community awareness and understanding of the effect of HIV epidemic on Latinos in the U.S. and the importance of community efforts to prevent HIV infection in the community. Finally, as they finished their training, community health workers were being integrated into ongoing Project Salud' research and prevention activities such as development of research instruments, recruitment of study participants, delivery of survey and intervention instruments, and dissemination of information. Following an increasingly relevant strategy of training community members in underserved communities and employing them as CHWs [57-59], LMW-HIVP trainees are playing a key role in disseminating the knowledge and skills they received as part of their training to promote health, prevent HIV infection, and reduce health disparities in the Latino migrant community. As members of the community, training participants possess an intimate understanding of community social networks, communicate in a similar language, and recognize and incorporate cultural elements to promote health and health outcomes within their community. However, research and prevention strategies not only require knowledge and skills but the material means to apply them. Project Salud, in partnership with the Farmworker Association of Florida, has created a permanent research facility in the Association's offices in Homestead that houses many of the activities related to our current project and our plans for future ones.

Researchers should be drawn to CBPR for its potential to promote public health in a way that embraces reciprocity with community members and engenders mutual ownership of the research process. Those of us who have been part of Project Salud feel that our efforts have contributed to improve HIV prevention in the LMW community. However, we have also encountered numerous challenges in actualizing a CBPR approach, particularly in terms of capacity building and sustainability. Despite these challenges, we feel that CBPR is the ideal approach to reach out to the Latino migrant worker community and elevate their voices while addressing the numerous and dire public health issues they face. As we move forward with our work, we are aware of these challenges but remain hopeful that CBPR holds great possibilities to improve health outcomes in the Latino migrant worker community.

REFERENCES

[1] HIV Surveillance Report, Vol. 23; February 2013. Centers for Disease Control and Prevention. Published: February 2015. Accessed: August 2015. URL: http://www.cdc.gov/hiv/pdf/g-l/hiv_surveillance_report_vol_25.pdf

[2] HIV Surveillance Supplemental Report, Vol. 17, No. 4; December 2012. Centers for Disease Control and Prevention. Published: November 2014. Accessed: August 2015. URL: http://www.cdc.gov/hiv/library/reports/surveillance/

[3] Fact Sheet: HIV in the United States. Centers for Disease Control and Prevention. Published: November 2013. Accessed: August 2015. URL: http://www.cdc.gov/hiv/pdf/statistics_basics_factsheet.pdf

[4] HIV Surveillance Supplemental Report, Vol. 18, No. 7; Published: October 2013. Centers for Disease Control and Prevention. Accessed: August 2015. URL: http://www.cdc.gov/hiv/pdf/surveillance_Report_vol_18_no_7.pdf

[5] Fact Sheet: HIV among Hispanics/Latinos in the United States and Dependent Areas. Centers for Disease Control and Prevention. Published: November 2013. Accessed: August 2015. URL: http://www.cdc.gov/hiv/pdf/risk_latino.pdf

[6] Soskolne V, Shtarkshall RA. Migration and HIV prevention programmes: Linking structural factors, culture, and individual behaviour--an Israeli experience. Soc Sci Med 2002; 55(8):1297-1307.

[7] Shtarkshall, R., & Soskolne, V. Migrant populations and HIV/AIDS: The development and implementation of programmes: theory, methodology and practice. UNESCO UNAIDS, 2000.

[8] Organista PB, Organista KC, Soloff PR. Exploring AIDS-related knowledge, attitudes, and behaviors of female Mexican migrant workers. *Health Soc. Work*. 1998; 23(2):96-103.

[9] Aranda-Naranjo B, Gaskins S. HIV/AIDS in migrant and seasonal farm workers. *J. Assoc. Nurses AIDS Care*. 1998; 9(5):80-3.

[10] Fernandez MI, Collazo JB, Hernandez N, et al. Predictors of HIV risk among Hispanic farm workers in South Florida: women are at higher risk than men. *AIDS Behav*. 2004; 8(2):165-74.

[11] Hernandez MT, Lemp GF, Castañeda X, et al. HIV/AIDS among Mexican migrants and recent immigrants in California and Mexico. *J. Acquir. Immune Defic. Syndr.* 2004; 37(4):s203-17.

[12] Sanchez MA, Lemp GF, Rodriguez-Magis C, Bravo-Garcia W, Carter S, Ruiz JD. The epidemiology of HIV among Mexican Migrants and recent immigrants in California and Mexico. *J. Acquir. Immune Defic. Syndr.* 2004; 37(4):s204-14.

[13] HIV Behavioral Interventions for Hispanics/Latinos in the US: A Meta-Analytic Review. Center for Disease Control and Prevention. Accessed: August 2015 URL: http://www.cdcnpin.org/scripts/HispanicLatino/files/herbst_latinoconsult.pdf

[14] Deren S, Sheldin M, Decena CU, Mino M. Research challenges to the study of HIV/AIDS among migrant and immigrant Hispanic populations in the United States. *J. Urban Health.* 2005; 82(2):iii13-25.

[15] Mishra SI, Conner RF. Evaluation of an HIV prevention program among Latino farmworkers. In Mishra SI, Conner RF, Magaña JR, eds. AIDS crossing borders: The spread among migrant Latino. Colorado: Westview Press, 1996.

[16] Weatherby NL, McCoy HV, Bletzer KV, et al. Sexual activity and HIV among drug users: Migrant workers and their sexual partners in southern Florida. *Florida Journal of Public Health.* 1995:7(1):22-6.

[17] McCoy HV, McCoy CB, Lai S. Effectiveness of HIV interventions among women drug users. *Women Health.* 1998:27(1-2):49-69.

[18] Kumpfer KL, Alvarado R, Smith P, Bellamy N. Cultural sensitivity in universal family-based prevention interventions. *Prev. Sci.* 2002; 3: 241-4.

[19] Bernal G, Saez-Santiago. Culturally centered psychosocial interventions. *J. Comm. Psych.* 2006; 34:121-32.

[20] McCoy HV, McCoy CB, Lai S, et al. Behavior changes among crack-using rural and urban women. *Subst. Use Misuse.* 1999:34(4-5):667-84.

[21] Weatherby NL, McCoy HV, Bletzer KV, et al. Immigration and HIV among migrant workers in rural southern Florida. *J. Drug Issues.* 1997; 27(1):155-72.

[22] Rao P, Hancy K, Velez M, et al. HIV/AIDS and farmworkers in the US. Farmworker Justice, 2008.

[23] Organista KC, Carrillo H, Ayala G. HIV prevention with Mexican migrants. Review, critique and recommendations. *J. Acquir. Immune Defic. Syndr.* 2004; 37(4):S227-39.

[24] Vega WA, Rodriguez MA, Gruskin, E. Health disparities in the Latino population. *Epidemiol. Rev*. 2009; 31:99-112.

[25] Arcury TA, Austin CK, Quandt SA, et al. Enhancing community participation in intervention research: farmworkers and agricultural chemicals in North Carolina. *Health Educ. Behav*. 1999; 26(4):563-78.

[26] Minkler M, Wallerstein N. eds. Community-based participatory research for health: From process to outcomes. 2nd Ed. San Francisco, CA: Jossey-Bass, 2008.

[27] Eng E, Parker E. Measuring community competence in the Mississippi Delta: the interface between program evaluation and empowerment *Health Education and Behavior*. 1994; 21(2):199-220.

[28] Rhodes SD, Hergenrather KC, Montaño J, et al. Using community-based participatory research to develop an intervention to reduce HIV and STD infections among Latino men. *AIDS Educ. Prev*. 2006; 18(5):375-89.

[29] Andrews OJ, Newman DS, Meadows O, et al. Partnership readiness for community-based participatory research. *Health Educ. Res*. 2010; PMID: 20837654.

[30] Eisinger A, Senturia KD. Doing community-driven research: A description of Seattle partners for healthy communities. *J. Urban Health*. 2001; 78(3): 519-34.

[31] Hughes D, DuMont K. Using focus groups to facilitate culturally anchored research. *American J. Comm. Psych*. 1993; 21:775-806.

[32] Morgan, DL. The focus group guidebook. Thousand Oaks, CA: Sage, 1993.

[33] Asbury, J. Overview of focus group research. *Qual. Health Res*. 1995; 5:414-20.

[34] Vanoss Marin, B. HIV prevention in the Hispanic community: Sex, culture, and empowerment. *J. Transcultural Nursing*. 2003; 14(3):186-92.

[35] U.S. Census Bureau. State and county quick facts, Homestead, Florida. Data derived from Population Estimates. Accesed 2011 August 22. URL: http://quickfacts.census.gov/qfd/states/12/1232275.html

[36] Bandura, A. Social cognitive theory and exercise of control over HIV infection. In: DiClemente RJ, Peterson J, (Eds). Preventing AIDS: Theories and Methods of Behavioral Interventions. New York, NY: Plenum Publishing; 1994:25-59.

[37] Baldwin J. Using peer education approaches in HIV/AIDS programs for youth: A review of the literature. *Peer Facilitator Q*. 1995; 12:34-37.

[38] Latkin, CA. Outreach in natural settings: the use of peer leaders for HIV prevention among injecting drug users' networks. *Public Health Reports.* 1998; 113(Suppl. 1):151-159.

[39] Morisky DE. Ang A. Coly A & Tiglao TV. A model HIV/AIDS risk reduction program in the Phillipines: a comprehensive community-based approach through participatory action research. *Health Promotion International*. 2004; 19(1):69-76.

[40] Morisky DE. Ebin VJ. The effectiveness of peer education STD/HIV prevention. In: Alex S, Kar S & Alcalay R (Eds.). Health Communication: A Multicultural Perspective. Thousand Oaks, CA: Sage Publications, Inc. 2004:211-234.

[41] Pearlman DN, Camberg L, Wallace LJ, Symons P & Finison L. Tapping youth as agents for change: evaluation of a peer leadership HIV/AIDS intervention. *Journal of Adolescent Health* 2002; 31(1):31-39.

[42] Kalichman S, Somlai A, & Sikkema K. Community involvement in HIV-AIDS prevention. In: Schneiderman N, Gentry J, da Silva JM, Speers M & Tomes H (Eds.), Integrating Behavioral and Social Sciences with Public Health. Washington, DC: *American Psychological Association.* 2001: 85-102.

[43] Miller WR & Rollnick S. Motivational Interviewing: Preparing People for Change. New York, NY: Guilford Press. 2002.

[44] Kalichman, S. C., Cherry, C., & Browne-Sperling, F. Effectiveness of a video-based motivational skills building HIV risk-reduction intervention for inner-city African American men. *Journal of Consulting and Clinical Psychology.* 1999; 67:959-966.

[45] Piantadosi S. Clinical Trials: A Methodologic Perspective. New York, NY: John Wiley & Sons. 1997.

[46] Sánchez J, De La Rosa M, Serna CA. Project Salud: Efficacy of a community-based HIV prevention intervention for Hispanic migrant workers in South Florida. *AIDS Ed. & Prev*. 2013; 25(5):363–375.

[47] Eisinger A, Senturia KD. Doing community-driven research: A description of Seattle partners for healthy communities. *J Urban Health.* 2001; 78(3): 519-34.

[48] Calleson DC, Seifer SD, Maurana C. Forces Affecting Community Involvement of AHCs: Perspectives of Institutional and Faculty Leaders. *Acad Med.* 2002; 77(1):72-81.

[49] Examining Community-Institutional Partnerships for Prevention Research Group. Building and Sustaining Community-Institutional

Partnerships for Prevention Research: Findings from a National Collaborative. *J. Urban Health*. 2006; 83(6):989-1003.

[50] Freire P. Education for Critical Consciousness. New York: Seabury Press, 1973.

[51] Beeker C, Guenther-Grey C, Raj A. Community empowerment paradigm drift and the primary prevention of HIV/AIDS. *Soc. Sci. Med.* 1998; 47:831–842.

[52] Wallerstein N. Powerlessness, empowerment, and health: Implications for health promotion programs. *Am. J. Health Promot*. 1992; 6:197–205.

[53] Wallerstein N, Baker R. Labor education programs in health and safety. *Occup. Med. State Art Rev*. 1994; 9:305–320.

[54] Freeman ER, Brugge D, Bennet-Bradley WM, Levy JI, Carrasco ER. Challenges of conducting community-based participatory research in Boston's neighborhoods to reduce disparities in asthma. *J. Urban Health.* 2006; 83(6): 1013-1021.

[55] Strickland, CJ. Challenges in Community-Based Participatory Research Implementation: Experiences in Cancer Prevention with Pacific Northwest American Indian Tribes. *Cancer Control*, 2006; 13:230-236.

[56] Israel BA, Eng E, Schultz AJ, Parker, EA eds. Methods in Community-Based Participatory Research for Health. San Francisco, Calif: Jossey-Bass; 2005.

[57] Parker EA, Schulz EA, Israel BA, et al. Worker Partnership: Community-Based Lay Health Advisor Intervention in an Urban Area. *Health Educ. Behav*. 1998; 25(1):24-45.

[58] Jackson EJ, Parks CP. Recruitment and Training Issues from Selected Lay Health Advisor Programs among African Americans: A 20-Year Perspective. *Health Educ. Behav*. 1997; 24: 418-431.

[59] Rhodes SD, Foley KL, Someta CS, et al. Lay Health Advisor Interventions Among Hispanics/Latinos: A Qualitative Systematic Review. *Am. J. Prev. Med.* 2007; 33(5):418-27.

In: Capacity Building
Editor: Diane Brown

ISBN: 978-1-63483-995-2

Chapter 4

MEASURING COMMUNITY CAPACITIES WITH "KEQ": PSYCHOMETRIC TESTS RESULTS FOR A NEWLY DEVELOPED INSTRUMENT FOR HEALTH PROMOTION PROGRAMS IN GERMANY

Stefan Nickel**, Waldemar Süß and Alf Trojan
University Medical Center Hamburg, Department of Medical Sociology
Martinistraße, Hamburg, Germany

ABSTRACT

Introduction: "KEQ" (Kapazitätsentwicklung im Quartier [Capacity Building in Residential Areas/Neighborhoods]) is the name of a newly developed questionnaire for measuring community capacities considered relevant to health. It is particularly based on the preliminary work of Glenn Laverack and Ronald Labonte who originally differentiated between nine domains of community capacities. KEQ is the first measurement instrument for capacity building in Germany, and can be seen as an intermediate outcome parameter for health promotion programs and activities at the community-level. This research was funded by the Federal Ministry of Education and Research.

* Email: nickel@uke.de

Objectives: The general research goal was the development of an instrument for the long-term assessment of health promotion activities in disadvantaged neighborhoods. This chapter will start presenting the neighborhood and health promotion program as the context for developing the instrument. The major section will focus on the psychometric testing of the KEQ instrument according to the classical test theory (objectivity, reliability, and validity). Practicality was analyzed in terms of length of time taken to complete the questionnaire, and number of missing values.

Methods: Surveys were conducted to measure community capacities, each with 40 to 60 stakeholders or change agents, from five socially disadvantaged areas in Hamburg, Germany, at different points in time. The KEQ instrument consists of five domains (participation, local leadership, available resources, networking and cooperation, health care) as a 51 item long-form. (A 31 item short-form is currently under development.) Analyses comprised both descriptive and inference statistics.

Results: Psychometric findings on the basis of N=235 respondents (37% out of 638 in total) permit the application of KEQ in small urban communities (about 3,000 to 20,000 residents). Cronbach's alpha as a coefficient of internal consistency ranged between .82 ("available resources") and .94 ("health care"). The results of the five domains of community capacity and their changes over time can best be depicted in spider diagrams. This form of presentation proved to be highly suitable for feed-back to agents of change in the residential areas involved.

Conclusion: The modular design of the questionnaire allows its flexible use for various assessment goals. Supposedly it is more suitable for measuring quality development than for evidence-producing outcome evaluation. Additional approaches are required to compensate for the possibly one-sided expert perspectives in the KEQ assessments (e.g., "triangulation" or "cross-examination" using groups of residents as informants). Further research is needed to study capacity building in association with final health outcomes.

1. Introduction

In addition to the empowerment of the individual, capacity building is described in the Jakarta Declaration of 1997 as one of the five priorities for leading health promotion into the 21st century. Under the heading "Increase Community Capacity and Empower the Individual" it was stated that the determinants of health are predominantly influenced by humans themselves. Being able to cope better with adverse determinants requires practical education, leadership training, and access to resources (WHO, 2009, p. 20). Meanwhile, these community capacities are applied as estimators for the sustainability of newly initiated developments in health promotion, for which no measurement had existed in Germany for a long time (Walter and Schwartz, 2003, p. 206). This methodological gap was closed in 2006 by "KEQ" (Kapazitätsentwicklung im Quartier/Capacity Building in Areas/ Neighborhoods) when the questionnaire was used for the "diagnosis of an urban area" called "Lenzsiedlung" [Lenz residential area] (Mossakowski et al., 2007). KEQ is the acronym of an instrument, newly developed by the Department of Medical Sociology of the University Medical Center Hamburg within the context of health promoting activities in the Lenzsiedlung neighborhood.

The starting point for the development of KEQ was the operationalization of "capacity building" defined by Labonte and Laverack (2000; 2001a/b)[1]. They describe approaches based on both quantitative and qualitative social research, and particularly recommend them for long-term effects (Labonte and Laverack, 2001a). Based on their preliminary work, the Department of Medical Sociology developed a standardized questionnaire through which community capacity can be assessed as an intermediate health parameter.

The questionnaire is addressed to professional actors from the social, educational and health care system. After its initial testing in 2006, the instrument was improved according to respondent recommendations (including additional criteria in the health domain and new wording of some items for better understanding). A reduction in the length of the instrument and the publication of supporting material for users of the instrument are under progress.

Unlike Labonte's and Laverack's approach to *initiate* capacity building, our approach is primarily used for the *measurement* of community capacities. The aim to develop a generic quantitative instrument posed us with special methodological problems: While Laverack and others needed a small number of active community members we needed a sufficiently large number of professional experts broadly informed about their neighborhood, even beyond their own special tasks. These are not easily found in any circumstances.

---

[1] In this chapter we cannot discuss the various overlaps and affinities of "capacity building" with similar approaches, especially "community development" (Jackson, Mitchell and Wright, 1989), "community organization" (Minkler and Wallerstein, 1997), "community empowerment" (Labonte, 1990; Maton and Salem, 1995), and also the overlapping concepts of "coalition building," "social capital," "social networking," "social mobilization" (Nutbeam, 1998).

The term "community" refers to a population in a socially and geographically defined area with all its residents, professional actors, structures, resources and competencies.

The general research goal was the development of a questionnaire for long-term assessments of health promotion programs in disadvantaged areas/neighborhoods. We will present the area and the health promotion program as the context for developing the instrument (2), the psychometric testing of the KEQ instrument according to the classical test theory (objectivity, reliability, validity and practicality) (3), sample results from using the instrument in the Lenzsiedlung and four other areas (4), and finally a discussion (5) and conclusion (6).

2. Setting of Research

Lenzsiedlung and the Health Promotion Program

The primary study took place in a densely populated tower block complex in Hamburg known as "Lenzsiedlung" in one of nine districts of the administrative unit Eimsbüttel.

The area/neighborhood was included in the Hamburg Senate program for "Social Urban Development" (since 2005 known as "Active Urban Development") in 2000, and remained so until the end of February 2007. According to the latest data approximately 3,000 people live there in total, of whom around 53 percent are female and around 29 percent under 18 years. Almost 60 per cent of the residents have an immigrant background. Another special feature of the area is that one out of three residents receives unemployment benefits (Arbeitslosengeld II/"Hartz IV").

In autumn 2003, a "round table" in the Lenzsiedlung was launched through an initiative of the local health authority. The round table continued to meet until mid-2012. At this round table the various organizations, institutions and individuals in the fields of health, social affairs and education held discussions and worked together: doctors, the youth welfare office, family midwife, maternity center, area office, community center, daycare center, educational counseling and many more (Mossakowski et al., 2007). The health authority, the initiator of health promotion in the Lenzsiedlung, simply took on the role of a secretary or coordinator. The round table consisted of the relevant health stakeholders, who saw themselves as representatives of the residents' interests.

In 2005, the disease prevention program "Lenzgesund" ["Lenzhealth"], focusing on children and their parents, was presented to the round table by the local health authority. It was approved, and since then has been implemented with the help of the round table and other cooperation partners. The core contents of the dynamic action approach were the organization and coordination of activities around pregnancy, birth and the first years of life, with the aims of improving the health situation of the residents and gaining their active participation.

The research tried to follow as closely as possible the key principles of community-based research, as described in a synthesis by Israel et al. (1998). According to the decision of the round table the complete program consisted of seven fields of action and two cross-sectional assignments, which had to be integrated in all fields of action (Lorentz and Trojan, 2013):

1. pregnancy/advice during that time
2. pregnancy/underage parents (services for adolescents)
3. postnatal support and help in the first year
4. vaccination
5. early childhood care
6. dental health care
7. diet, exercise and addiction

Cross-sectional assignments:

- health literacy of parents
- prevention of violence

In all fields of action the stakeholders began activities and projects at the neighborhood level directed to the target groups. Between 2005 and 2012 the Medical Department of Sociology conducted two consecutive accompanying research projects, funded by the Federal Ministry of Education and Research[2].

Four other areas/neighborhoods in Hamburg were also included in the study in a so-called transfer test, each representing different levels of neighborhood development. One area had long-standing, broad experience in

[2] Project 1: "Capacity Building" for prevention and health promotion in children and parents in a disadvantaged area. (5/2005 until 2/2009; grant agreement number: 01 EL 0414); Project 2: Evaluation of the prevention program "Lenzgesund." Transfer potential of an innovative evaluation instrument to measure capacity building. (3/2009 until 12/2012; grant agreement number: 01 EL 0812).

social and health-related neighborhood development activities ("Flüsseviertel and Lüdersring-Lüttkamp" in Hamburg-Lurup), and three areas did not have such experiences ("Essener Straße" in Hamburg-Langenhorn, "Hohenhorst" in Hamburg-Rahlstedt, "Steilshoop" in Hamburg-Wandsbek). All areas were characterized by the fact that a high proportion of socially disadvantaged people lived there, and that they had been included in the federal-state program "Social City" and/or the regional program for "Active Urban Development" (since mid-2007).

3. The Instrument and Its Psychometric Quality

Instrument

The newly developed instrument "KEQ" (Trojan and Nickel, 2013) is based on the preliminary work of Labonte and Laverack (see above) and other international studies and reviews (including Goodman et al. 1998; Hawe et al. 2000; Bush et al. 2002; Kwan et al. 2003; Rifkin, 2003; Noack and Reis-Klingspiegl, 2006). After an in-depth discussion of the literature used by the research team and an exploratory assessment by nine experts from health science and practice in this field, a first version of the instrument was created. The adaptation to German conditions can predominately be seen as concretizing, bundling together, and accentuating the original themes.

The KEQ questionnaire consists of 51 statements about the fulfilment of criteria for building community capacities in five domains: participation, local leadership, available resources, networking and cooperation, and health care (see Appendix).

The first version additionally contained 15 open-ended questions, but a 31 item short-form without open-ended questions is currently under construction. All standardized items have the same 5-point answer scale: 1 "(nearly) not achieved" – 2 "slightly achieved" – 3 "partly achieved" – 4 "widely achieved" – 5 "(nearly) completely achieved." Users can also tick the box "cannot assess." Through addition and division by the number of valid items, the sub-scales for the five dimensions can be seen in the same range. The prerequisite for this calculation is that a person answers at least half the items for a dimension.

Study Procedure

The KEQ surveys in the Lenzsiedlung and in the other four disadvantaged areas in Hamburg were carried out in the same way between 2005 and 2012 (Nickel and Trojan, 2013a and 2013b):

- presentation of the research project in the local working groups or neighborhood committees (e.g., round table "Lenzgesund")
- creating a list of 40-60 key informants from the health, social and educational institutions in or around the area with the help of our local cooperation partners
- sending out the questionnaires with an invitation letter and additionally offering financial incentives (20-30 Euro per person)
- reminders approximately 3-4 weeks later
- non-responder analysis (telephone call)
- data analysis, reporting and feedback to the community and the round table

Statistical analysis of KEQ results is based on descriptive methods and coefficients (means, frequency distributions, crosstabs), supplemented by significance tests such as the t-test for independent samples, analysis of variance (ANOVA) and bivariate correlations. We used the internationally recommended "spider-web" mapping technique for visualization of the quantitative results with regard to capacity building (Labonte and Laverack, 2001b, pp. 130 f.).

Respondents

The names of the settings, the survey periods and the response rates of the different surveys are shown in Table 1. Total responses to the survey were 235 out of 638 distributed questions, which means an average response rate of 37% (depending on the neighborhood and time of inquiry, between 26% and 56%).

The group of respondents included 52 (28%) professionals from the public health service or other local authorities; 64 (34%) were social and educational workers (area management, kindergarten, school, private agencies); "other" institutions (27%) were another large proportion of respondents – in contrast to health professionals, who participated only slightly. The majority of respondents were female (60%) and lived neither in nor near the area (85%).

Some 80% described their knowledge of the neighborhood in general as "good" or "very good," and 49% knew the local health sector as well.

Table 1. Settings and Respondents to the KEQ Surveys (Response Rates in Parenthesis)

Area/neighborhood in Hamburg	Period of inquiry	Number of inquiries	Respondents (N and %)
Lenzsiedlung	05/2006-11/2011	3	27/20/24 (56%/42%/50%)
Flüsseviertel and Lüdersring-Lüttkamp †	10/2007-04/2009	2	23/15 (40%/26%)
Essener Straße	10/2007-11/2010	2	26/26 (45%/31%)
Hohenhorst	10/2007-11/2010	2	15/17 (36%/33%)
Steilshoop	04/2009-04/2012	2	25/19 (32%/28%)

† The two areas of the Hamburgian district Lurup are treated here as one neighborhood.

Psychometric Quality of the Instrument

The psychometric quality of the instrument was tested according to the methods of classical test theory (Lienert and Raatz, 1998; Bortz and Döring, 2006). Characteristic features of this theory are certain assumptions about the quality criteria of a test or measuring instrument: objectivity, reliability and validity. We also analyzed factors potentially influencing the assessment of community capacities and the practicality of the instrument (time for completion, totality of missing values).

Objectivity and Practicality

The above-mentioned standardized steps for carrying out a KEQ survey ensure good *implementation objectivity*, but other elements of implementation may threaten the results, in particular incomplete anonymity, a bias due to social desirability, the approval of questions regardless of their content ("acquiescence") and/or explicit denial of a response (Schnell, Hill and Esser, 1993, pp. 361 ff.). It is critical to note here that surveys using KEQ are based on the responses of those who are strongly involved in the process and thus may give distorted assessments; however, this can result in both overly positive and overly negative views compared to more neutral evaluators.

Evaluation objectivity can be taken for granted if the relevant parts of the questionnaire remain unchanged, and the item and sub-scale scores are charged according to the general statistics for the social sciences. For the purpose of analyzing KEQ we have developed a computerized program that supports both the calculation of scales and their analysis (www.uke.de/institute/medizin-soziologie/index_28299.php).

With regard to *practicality*, ambiguous conclusions have to be drawn. On the one hand the investment of time, money and personnel for the implementation and evaluation are within an acceptable range, especially if the required technical and organizational know-how is available, but there are also disadvantages such as a relatively small basis for sampling, amount of time spent on personal motivation, and rather low response rates.

Subsequent qualitative analysis of non-respondents revealed a high proportion of people who did not consider themselves informed enough to give an adequate assessment (including many professionals who did not directly work in the neighborhood or were responsible for larger areas). Others were not reachable or not interested in the survey, despite multiple attempts to motivate them.

Item Analysis

Descriptive characteristics of the items are shown in Table 2. The proportion of missing values varies from 3.8 to 50.0% and is not always in an acceptable range (< 20%); particularly for the items in the "health care" dimension; this proportion was high due to the frequent use of the response category "cannot judge." It is also noticeable that almost all item raw scores in the first four subscales, but only two items in the fifth sub-scale, are left-skewed in distribution. The most obvious right-skewness in one dimension appears in Item 50 ("There are enough offers to promote and protect the health of men"). Unlike the other items, here negative assessments prevail from the perspective of the interviewees.

The item difficulties and item-total correlations (including the corrected item-total correlations) for each item were calculated. The *item difficulty*, the percentage of achieved from maximum achievable scores, involves how "difficult" or "easy" it is to answer an item. Generally, item difficulties between .20 to .80 are accepted (Bortz and Döring, 2006, p. 218). The *item-total correlation* provides information about how well the total test result is predictable from responses to a single item, and is defined as the correlation between an item and the total value in each dimension (A to E). As the overall test value is computed with this item, corrected item-total correlations were calculated on the basis of total test scores that allow the current item disregarded (marked in the table with a point). The discriminatory power for most of the items can be regarded as high, with values above .50 (ibid., p. 219).

Table 2. Descriptive Measures and Item-Total Correlations for All Items (n=235)

Item no.	Missing (%)	Mean	SD	Skewness	Difficulty	Item-total correlations †				
						A	B	C	D	E
1.	11.1	3.02	.74	-.11	60.5	.57•	.31	.32	.26	.20
2.	8.9	3.33	.77	.17	66.6	.59•	.37	.44	.20	.28
3.	14.0	2.99	1.04	-.05	59.7	.45•	.34	.36	.23	.47
4.	12.3	2.47	.83	.13	49.3	.58•	.25	.31	.31	.10
5.	11.5	2.94	.83	-.09	58.8	.69•	.34	.39	.33	.15
6.	14.5	2.67	.95	.03	53.3	.69•	.38	.39	.43	.24
7.	10.2	3.45	1.04	-.36	68.9	.59•	.50	.40	.46	.32
8.	13.2	3.47	1.12	-.48	69.3	.60•	.50	.34	.43	.30
9.	14.0	3.33	1.19	-.44	66.6	.65•	.67	.53	.40	.45
10.	5.1	3.93	.83	-.44	78.7	.28	.38•	.27	.40	.16
11.	25.1	2.65	1.15	-.13	53.0	.36	.53•	.41	.35	.62
12.	15.3	3.69	.97	-.73	73.8	.44	.59•	.33	.38	.41
13.	11.5	3.53	1.06	-.39	70.7	.63	.80•	.56	.50	.58
14.	18.3	3.92	1.01	-.94	78.4	.34	.60•	.40	.45	.38
15.	20.0	3.75	1.41	-.87	75.0	.42	.59•	.57	.35	.41
16.	30.2	3.18	1.25	-.18	63.7	.42	.69•	.52	.41	.37
17.	15.3	3.68	.95	-.40	73.7	.44	.65•	.48	.47	.41
18.	33.2	2.87	1.20	.05	57.5	.40	.62•	.37	.43	.49
19.	16.2	2.74	.95	.02	54.7	.20	.34	.40•	.32	.23
20.	6.0	3.37	1.02	-.13	67.3	.28	.29	.58•	.18	.33
21.	16.2	3.25	1.13	-.43	65.1	.22	.31	.56•	.23	.34
22.	20.9	3.38	1.09	-.43	67.6	.37	.53	.42•	.33	.52
23.	3.8	3.94	.92	-.87	78.8	.40	.48	.43•	.48	.27

Item no.	Missing (%)	Mean	SD	Skewness	Difficulty	Item-total correlations †				
						A	B	C	D	E
24.	14.0	3.00	1.09	-.15	59.9	.38	.46	.51•	.32	.55
25.	20.9	3.06	.84	-.07	61.3	.39	.47	.55•	.43	.32
26.	19.1	2.90	.76	.10	58.0	.39	.32	.38•	.31	.28
27.	16.6	3.36	.89	-.59	67.1	.36	.19	.36•	.26	.27
28.	11.9	3.91	1.07	-.12	58.2	.45	.44	.63•	.27	.54
29.	15.3	1.93	1.05	.84	38.7	.24	.26	.52•	.26	.30
30.	20.4	3.79	.87	-.47	75.8	.39	.43	.32	.81•	.27
31.	10.6	3.62	.88	-.26	72.5	.28	.31	.33	.58•	.20
32.	14.5	3.74	.92	-.58	74.8	.35	.37	.35	.68•	.29
33.	22.6	3.25	.83	-.13	64.9	.30	.44	.38	.66•	.35
34.	31.1	3.16	1.01	-.22	63.2	.33	.45	.43	.64•	.35
35.	46.4	3.06	1.05	-.24	61.1	.28	.45	.38	.67•	.37
36.	24.3	3.61	.90	-.61	72.1	.39	.42	.26	.76•	.21
37.	23.0	3.65	.90	-.53	73.0	.35	.47	.38	.71•	.28
38.	19.1	3.48	.92	-.37	69.7	.50	.55	.38	.68•	.36
39.	27.2	3.24	1.11	-.33	64.8	.45	.46	.42	.55•	.42
40.	25.0	2.79	1.23	.18	55.8	.25	.33	.40	.20	.61•
41.	30.8	2.88	1.20	.11	57.6	.26	.33	.40	.31	.63•
42.	39.9	2.69	1.29	.28	53.8	.41	.52	.47	.34	.78•
43.	38.0	3.23	.97	-.33	64.7	.26	.44	.39	.32	.68•
44.	36.5	2.62	1.33	.19	52.4	.24	.51	.51	.37	.76•
45.	35.1	2.60	1.13	.18	52.0	.40	.54	.46	.42	.83•
46.	36.1	2.98	1.21	-.32	59.5	.55	.60	.47	.54	.66•
47.	50.0	2.70	1.15	.14	54.0	.34	.47	.35	.37	.66•
48.	26.9	2.61	1.13	.08	52.2	.39	.50	.52	.26	.83•
49.	35.1	2.59	1.14	.10	51.7	.41	.49	.56	.36	.76•
50.	48.6	2.15	1.17	.81	43.0	.34	.38	.33	.28	.61•
51.	32.7	2.54	1.18	.12	50.7	.33	.43	.46	.34	.79•

† A = Participation (item 1-9), B = Local leadership (10-18), C = Available resources (19-29), D = Networking and cooperation (30-39), E = Health care (40-51).

• corrected item-total correlations (r_{it}) for scale-related items; elsewise bivariate correlations (Pearson).

The item-total correlations between the items and all other dimensions are shown in the five columns in the right half of the table. It is expected that the correlation of an item with its own scale is higher than with a different scale. This criterion is well fulfilled for the items of scales A = "participation" (no. 1-9), B = "local leadership" (10-18), D = "networking and cooperation" (30-39) and E = "health care" (40-51). The item-total correlations of items from scale C = "available resources" (19-29) with the other scales, however, were not satisfactory. Here the elimination or revision of some items (e.g., no. 22, 23, 24) could possibly improve the test statistics.

Reliability

The reliability of the five subscales of KEQ was checked using Cronbach's alpha and Spearman-Brown's split-half coefficient. Internal consistency ranges from .82 to .94 and is without exception satisfactory (see Cronbach's alpha in Table 3). The split-half coefficients differ according to Spearman-Brown, as expected, only slightly from the corresponding alpha coefficients and can also be evaluated as satisfactory. The reliability test showed, moreover, that the alpha coefficients could not be increased by the removal of an item (without table).

A test-retest with a short time interval between test and retest, as required for the testing of the stability of variables, was inappropriate due to the embedding of our study in ongoing activities to improve capacity building in the neighborhood. The dubious assumption that the "true" values between two or more measurements remain unchanged is not applicable in the context of interventions for change.

Table 3. Measures and Reliability of the KEQ Subscales (n = 235)

Subscale	Missing †	Mean ‡	SD	Skewness	Alpha #	r_{tt} #
Participation	10.6%	3.08	.65	-.45	.86	.82
Local leadership	13.2%	3.49	.80	-.37	.87	.74
Available resources	6.4%	3.08	.59	-.12	.82	.78
Networking and cooperation	17.0%	3.50	.68	-.64	.91	.87
Health care	32.2%	2.70	.95	.31	.94	.89

† Missing values: less than 50% items per dimension.
‡ Range: 1 "(nearly) not achieved" to 5 "(nearly) completely achieved."
# Reliability: Cronbach's alpha; split-half-coefficient r_{tt} (Spearman-Brown).

The intercorrelations of sub-scales are moderate to high, an indication that the five domains are not completely independent (see Table 4). All inter-correlations, however, are smaller than the coefficients of the internal consistency (diagonal in Table 4): the diversity of community capacities apparently exceeds the similarity of indicators of the construct.

Table 4. Intercorrelations of the KEQ Subscales (Cronbach's alpha in parenthesis)

Subscale	Participation	Local leadership	Available resources	Networking and cooperation	Health care
Participation	(.86)				
Local leadership	.59	(.87)			
Available resources	.54	.62	(.82)		
Networking and cooperation	.49	.58	.50	(.91)	
Health care	.43	.57	.58	.41	(.94)

Note: All correlations (Pearson) are highly significant ($p \leq .001$).

Table 5. Confounding Effects on KEQ Assessments and Practicality of the Instrument (n = 235)

	Assessments of KEQ domains #					Practicality	
	A	B	C	D	E	Time of completion	Number of missing values
Analysis of variance (Eta): †							
Affiliation	.24	.19	.30	.28	.30	.22	.32
Sex	.03	.14	.01	.08	.09	.04	.05
Living close to the area	.25**	.27**	.10	.14	.29**	.13	.12
Correlations (Pearson's r): ‡							
Knowledge about the area in general	.06	-.07	.00	-.02	-.18*	.22**	-.51**
Knowledge about the health sector of the area	.10	.06	-.03	-.02	.10	.13	-.28**

A = Participation, B = Local leadership, C = Available resources, D = Networking and cooperation, E = Health care.

† Eta ≥ .10 "small," ≥ .24 "medium," ≥ .37 "large" effect size.

‡ Pearson's r ≥ .10 "small," ≥ .30 "medium," ≥ .50 "large" effect size.

* $p \leq .05$ (significant); ** $p \leq .01$ (very significant),

Confounding Factors

By means of variance analysis and bivariate correlations we could examine the extent to which confounders (i.e., institutional affiliation, sex, living close to the area, general and health-related knowledge about the neighborhood) affect both stakeholder assessments of the KEQ domains, and the practical feasibility of the instrument. The results of these calculations are summarized in Table 5.

On the whole, significant differences are rare, and the effect sizes in the analyses are usually in the small to mid-range, however, two results are worth noting: firstly, community capacities in three domains (participation, local leadership, health care) are judged more positively the farther away respondents live from the neighborhood; and secondly, the better the knowledge about a neighborhood in general and/or with regard to the local health sector, the lower the number of missing values and the longer it takes to answer the questionnaire. Both results are clearly plausible.

4. Some Initial Experiences with the Capacity Building Measurement

The following illustrates the results for the development of sustainable structures and competences using the example of Lenzsiedlung. The quantitative results provide information about the weaknesses and strengths of the area's development that can be stated in the observed 10 year period between 2001 and 2011. We will also present some results for the four other neighborhoods examined in our study.

Developments in the Lenzsiedlung over Time

The results for the five domains of capacity building in the Lenzsiedlung over time are summarized in a spider-web diagram (see Figure 1). The situation in 2001 – the beginning of first health-promoting activities in this neighborhood – could only be assessed retrospectively (included in the first survey in 2006). In spite of methodological problems, this measurement has to be regarded as a "baseline": the starting point for subsequent developments (T0).

The overall positive results can mainly be attributed to the generally positive "climate" of neighborhood development and health promotion, and to the strong commitment and the perseverance of individual stakeholders from the areas of health, education and social services.

Complementary positive developments show up in the field of "participation" - understood as the active engagement of residents in community life (e.g., visits to information events or neighborhood festivals, use of public services). This result and positive assessments in the areas of "local leadership" and "networking and cooperation" are predominantly based on the information, coordination and activation work of three infrastructural pillars: the association for children, youth and community named "Lenzsiedlung e.V.," the neighborhood office of the area management, and the Lenzgesund round table.

The process of capacity development appears to have entered a consolidation phase. The T2 and T3 surveys (with somewhat lower response rates than at T1) continue to show some growth (e.g., in the dimension "health care") or remain at the same level (for example in the dimension "available resources"). The spider-web chart demonstrates quite well what is felt in thc community, too, that after the 10 year phase of activities, one can speak of a stable structure and capacity building in the Lenzsiedlung.

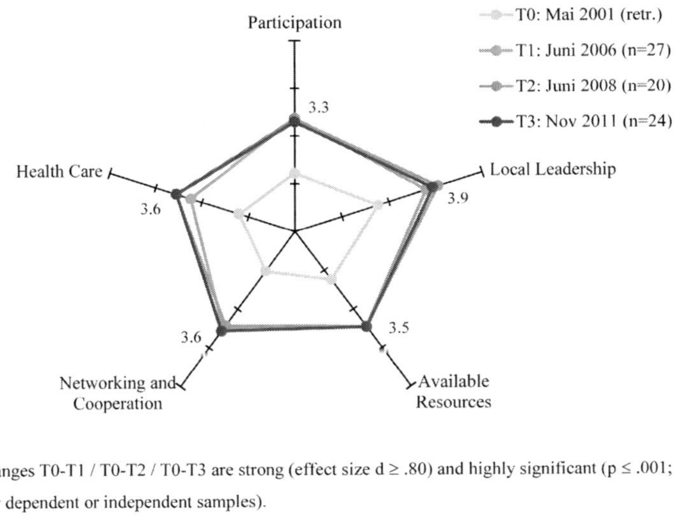

†All changes T0-T1 / T0-T2 / T0-T3 are strong (effect size d $\geq$ .80) and highly significant ($p \leq .001$; t-test for dependent or independent samples).

Figure 1. Capacity Building in the Lenzsiedlung over Time (means: 1 = worst, 5 = best) †.

There were two additional questions in the final KEQ survey (2011) in order to indirectly validate the results, particularly with respect to the KEQ scale "health": The first question asked whether the parts of their work relating to prevention and health promotion within the participating organizations of the respondents had been increased during the past few years. The vast majority (79%) of respondents felt that their institution was "very much" (35%) or "somewhat" (44%) more strongly interested in prevention and health promotion; only 17% reported that they were unchanged and 4% that they had less interest.

The second question asked whether respondents believed that these parts of their work would be expanded in the future, would continue or become less. 57% believed that the shares of prevention and health promotion would increase in their institutions, and another 30% thought that they would remain unchanged. Only a small minority of 13% expected a decline in such activities. These results add to the evidence of sustainable capacity building activities of health promotion and prevention.

Using the Results at Item-Level

Stakeholders and professionals in the community appreciate spider-web presentation as a quick overview, but they also need feedback on results, which tell them more precisely where they do well and where it is necessary to redirect or adapt their activities in the future. For this purpose we presented ranked single item lists.

Looking first at the five best of the 51 single KEQ criteria rated in 2011, it is noticeable that many goals of both the prevention program and the program for social urban development were achieved quite well (e.g., promoting civic commitment, better information about area-related activities and services). Other positive changes were especially found in the "local leadership" scale. The strongest progress in this domain was that authorities and social institutions increasingly recognized and accepted their responsibility for the Lenzsiedlung. Significant improvements were made in the qualities of leadership; including social skills (e.g., democratic and integrative leadership), and monitoring skills (e.g., the documentation of activities in the Lenzsiedlung). Because the main goal of the surveys was the identification of critical points, we present the top five criteria with the greatest need for further efforts, as an example how this was communicated to the actors in the Lenzsiedlung (see Figure 2). Not all the problematic elements are easy to cope with, but in the second item of Figure 3 the information gathered was successfully used: there was critical assessment of criteria regarding the motivation of residents to take the initiative and more responsibility.

This lead to recommendations for the neighborhood management in the Lenzsiedlung (Mossakowski et al. 2006) and subsequently to more support for the small group of residents who were willing and able to permanently participate in citizen initiatives and projects. In the last phase of the prevention program significant progress could be seen in this regard.

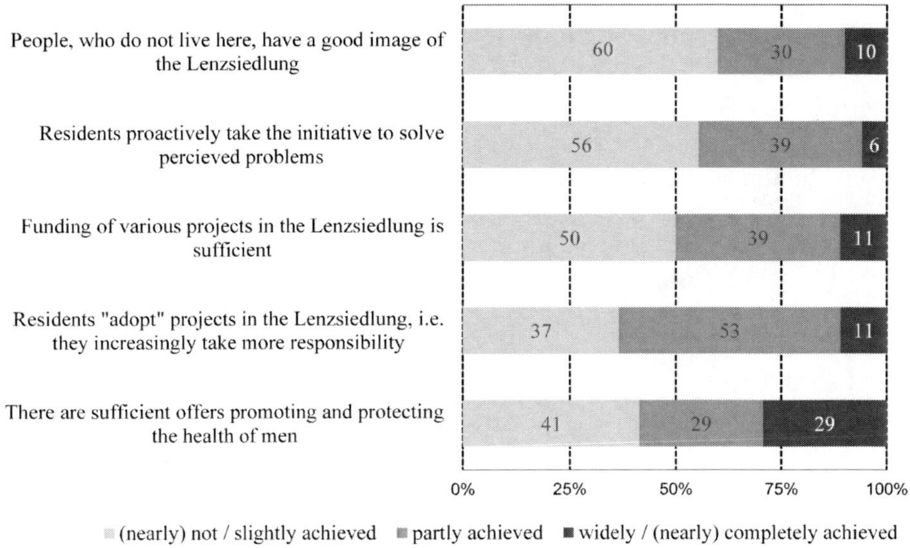

Figure 2. TOP-5 of Criteria with the *Greatest* Need for Action in the Lenzsiedlung in 2011 (n = 24).

Results from Other Neighborhoods

In addition to the long-term evaluation in the Lenzsiedlung, three areas (between 5,100 and 11,500 residents) and one district (19,300 residents) of Hamburg were researched at two points in time (T1 and T2), each representing different levels of social urban development and health promotion. With this transfer test we wanted to determine the extent to which the KEQ instrument can also be used in comparable areas in other phases of capacity building, and what problems it might encounter.

Type A: Areas with finished or consolidated projects of area-related health promotion

Results for the Flüsseviertel and Lüdersring-Lüttkamp areas are initially presented, which we have assigned as "Type A" of area-related health promotion (see Figure 3). The average scores for each domain of capacity building are depicted, with 5 being the best value again, and 1 the theoretical worst value. The relatively positive assessments apply to (almost) all domains. In comparison to the first survey interview, even a slight improvement in the dimensions of "participation" and "networking and cooperation" can be detected (mean: 3.3 and 3.8). This is an indication that despite the end of the area management the process of capacity building in Flüsseviertel and Lüdersring-Lüttkamp has entered a consolidation phase in which much is already running well and could be sustainably secured.

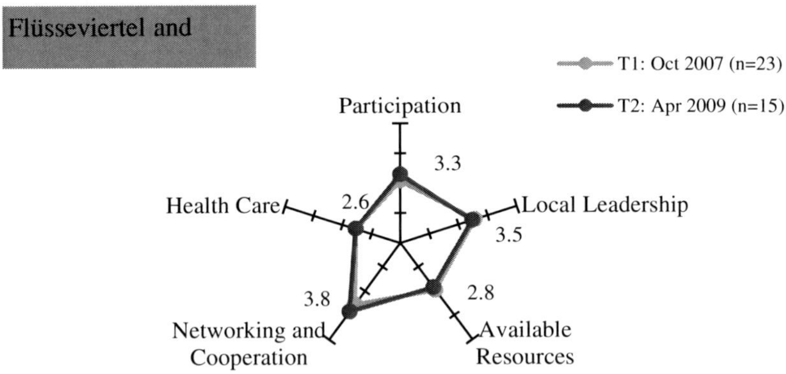

Figure 3. Capacity Building in Flüsseviertel and Lüdersing-Lüttkamp (means: 1 = worst, 5 = best).

Type B: Areas with no or few activities of area-related health promotion

Figure 4 summarizes the results of the KEQ measurements in the neighborhoods "Essener Straße" and "Hohenhorst," and the urban district "Steilshoop" in Hamburg. All three areas were initially attributed to a "Type B" of area-related health promotion, in which (as yet) no or only a few projects were developed and/or implemented. While the initial surveys (T1) were conducted some six to nine months after the start of the professional area management, the follow-up surveys (T2) were carried out about three years later. As expected, the assessments at T1 in most KEQ domains were rather low to medium for progress. In comparison, there is more or less strong progress in community capacities until T2. Depending on the area the positive changes are related to different domains, such as "health care" in Essener

Straße (2.9), "participation" in Hohenhorst (3.2) or "networking and cooperation" in Steilshoop (3.7). A direct comparison of the results between the neighborhoods, however, is difficult due to the different conditions (population structure, living environment, stakeholders, objectives, etc.) and activity priorities.

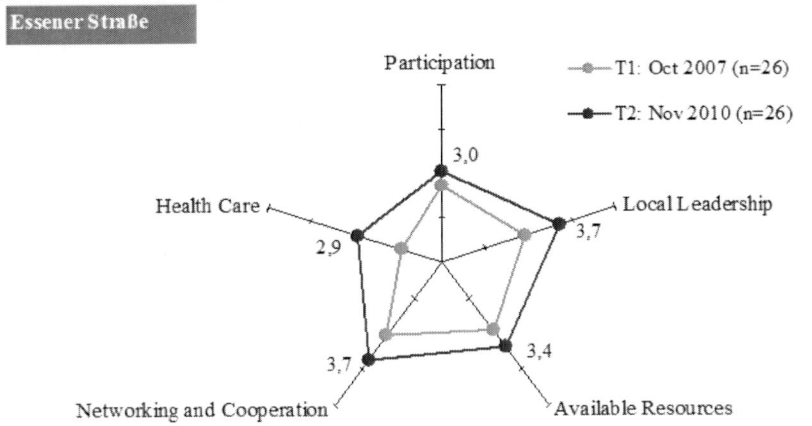

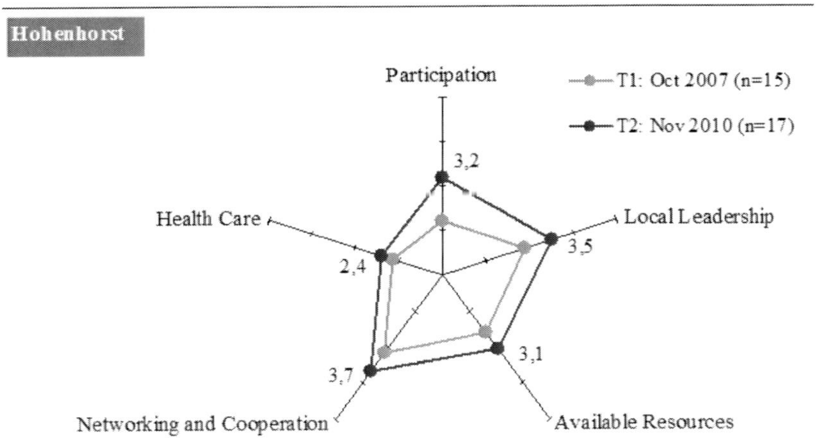

Figure 4. (Continued).

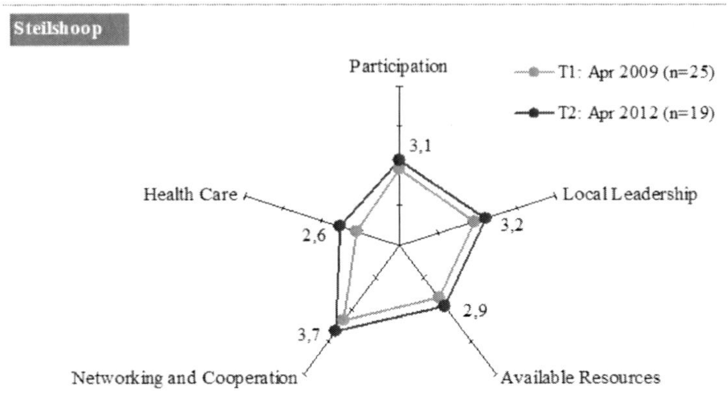

Figure 4. Capacity Building in Three Other Neighborhoods (means: 1 = worst, 5 = best).

Discussion

In the first section we will discuss KEQ as an instrument for the evaluation and quality development of community-level health promotion. The second section will reflect the psychometric results against the background of classical test theory and address limitations of our empirical results.

Instrument for Evaluation or Quality Development?

Is KEQ an appropriate tool for contributions to the evidence of interventions for improving health in individuals or in a population? On the one hand, measurement using KEQ seem to have great potential as an intermediate indicator of the success of multimodal health promotion programs. On the other hand, there are no empirically conclusive results that confirm the link between capacity building and health outcomes. Nickel and Trojan (2009) emphasize the need for further studies of the use of KEQ for purposes of conventional outcome evaluation.

The theoretical weight of health-related *community development* and community-related *health promotion* needs further discussion: To what extent should general issues of community development and participation be integrated or even dominate concrete health issues in the strict sense? To what extent can and should determinants of health from other policy sectors, such as urban development, social affairs, and youth, be explicitly raised? Which sizes of communities does the instrument really fit, when it has currently been used for districts and neighborhoods of between 3,000 and 20,000 inhabitants? - All these questions arise because the KEQ instrument not only measures the achievements of the specific program in the Lenzsiedlung, but is meant to be suitable for all contexts where a multimodal health promotion program in and with the setting "community" is put into practice. This further check is a research task, which we are just beginning.

According to our experience we believe KEQ to be more suitable for quality development than for evidence-producing evaluation aims. The instrument can "multi-functionally" impact positively on communities and their development (cf. the functions of evaluation according to Stockmann (2000)):

- *identification of strengths and weaknesses:* The questionnaire can "diagnose" the situation at the community level with regard to five key domains of capacity building. This knowledge can contribute to needs assessments preceding the health-promoting activities for an area.
- *monitoring function:* Through repeated KEQ-surveys and communicating the results to decision makers, the program can be better controlled and adapted to changing needs.
- *visualization of processes:* Progress and regress can easily be visualized using spider-net diagrams. Thus, actors and outsiders are quickly informed about general trends of the development.
- *legitimization of political and practical commitment:* Based on the KEQ results, necessary interventions can be justified more easily, and additional resources (money, information, rooms etc.) can be mobilized.
- *reduction of the complexity of impacting factors:* Many different factors influence processes of health promotion. It is often difficult to map the variety of factors with any differentiation and yet comprehensively. KEQ, with its five dimensions, permits a quick and transparent impression.
- *assessment of the sustainability of activities:* Through the repeated evaluation of structures and competences KEQ allows an estimation of the sustainability of health-promoting activities.

With the use of KEQ as part of an *optimization* paradigm (instead of in an *evaluation* paradigm for the intervention "multi-modal community-level health promotion"), the measurement of capacity building also comes close to the original approach of Laverack et al. (2008) as a *participation* tool in the so-called parallel tracking approach. Laverack et al. (ibid.) build upon earlier ideas which consider community capacity as the sum total of commitment, resources, and skills that a community can mobilize and deploy to address community problems and strengthen community assets and believe the concept to be fundamental to the concept of empowerment (Mayer, 1994).

The goal of creating a generic tool has been reached in principle; but the transferability to less socially disadvantaged and/or rural areas has not been tested (yet). Presumably the procedure is only applicable for certain (integrated) types of programs.

Test-Theoretical Findings

Overall, psychometric testing of the KEQ instrument shows good to acceptable test-theoretical properties of objectivity, reliability, and - with significantly greater restrictions - validity. Further analyses of the factorial validity, concurrent validity and predictive validity unfortunately could not be performed, on the one hand due to the large number of missing values and on the other hand due to missing external criteria.

The internal consistency in the coefficients of all five sub-scales is to a great deal distinctively above the required alpha value of .80 (Raithel, 2008). The items for each dimension were also mostly high in item-total correlation, which are usually greater than the correlations with the other dimensions. Only the scale "available resources" shows ambiguous results in this respect. The question of whether items have to be reformulated and/or the scale should be changed, could not be answered conclusively on the basis of the data currently available.

There are, however, a number of limitations for measurements with KEQ:

- The response rate remained below our expectations and what is desirable, despite great motivation efforts and the integration of our surveys into the ongoing activities of community development.
- A degree of achievement perceived from the perspective of some professionals as a "success," can be viewed from the perspective of other participants as "not enough" or even a "failure" (this seemed to

be the case in the item "information about activities and services in various languages"); this normative conditionality hinders a unique conception of "success."

- Statistical control of confounders remained necessarily incomplete and was so labor-intensive that it could not be achieved by local stakeholders without external research assistance.
- The interpretation of the measurements of change, including the question of the accountability of successes or failures in capacity building, remains fraught with uncertainty; and this problem may increase with the overlap of different programs for health promotion and social neighborhood development.

Despite these limitations (most are general difficulties in measuring change in community settings) the survey instrument's psychometric properties justify its use in complex health promotion approaches and continuous monitoring. The modular design of the questionnaire and its application, particularly in collaboration with professional community experts, allow flexible use, adapted to different settings. KEQ is the first survey instrument in the German language to assess capacity building in neighborhoods and communities. The long-term establishment of the instrument, however, requires a more intensive discussion not only about the opportunities, but also about the limits of the instrument and its applicability (cf. Liberato et al., 2011; Ogilvie et al., 2011).

To improve the response rate, which has been shown as a central problem of standardized surveys in our research project, the identification of as many actors and key persons as possible is recommended, including those from other sectors of community development. In our perception, the two most important barriers were the lack of more general knowledge about the neighborhood and the permanent overload of stakeholders with different responsibilities within their organizations.

In the future, the relationship between community capacity and specific endpoints of health promotion (life satisfaction, health status, self-efficacy etc.) could and should be studied more intensively using the KEQ instrument. Further research is needed on the sustainability of community capacity building. Additional approaches, such as "triangulation" or "cross-examination" are required to compensate the possibly one-sided expert perspective in the KEQ assessments. This includes key informant/expert interviews, focus groups of residents, content analysis of program plans and other forms of documentation (practitioner logs, minutes of meetings etc.) (cf.

Labonte and Laverack, 2001b, p. 130). In a current research project funded by the Federal Ministry of Education and Research we are also testing an audit, in which external peers in health promotion practice evaluate the KEQ results in the Lenzsiedlung, in order to validate our research instrument.[3]

Conclusion

The primary aim of KEQ, to measure community capacities over time, was achieved. The instrument is also suitable for local comparisons. It possibly needs to be adapted to local features for use in other contexts and countries. In addition to mapping the community capacities at a certain point in time it can be used for the continuous improvement of health promotion activities. The questionnaire can identify starting points for a continuous quality development of necessary interventions in a community, however, the methodological problems are not negligible and need further research.

Material for carrying out surveys with KEQ and analyzing the empirical data is available at: www.uke.de/institute/medizin-soziologie/index_77803.php [in German].

Appendix

The five scales for measuring "Kapazitätsentwicklung im Quartier" [Capacity Building in Residential Areas / Neighborhoods] (KEQ)

Scaling: (nearly) not achieved – slightly achieved – partly achieved – widely achieved – (nearly) completely achieved // cannot assess

A: Participation

1. Residents participate in social, political and cultural life of the area (e.g., membership in associations, self-help groups, neighborhood groups, citizen initiatives).

[3] Project: Long-term evaluation of complex community interventions for health promotion and prevention – An examination of community capacities ten years after the start of the "Program Lenzgesund" (10/2014 until 09/2017; grant agreement number: 01 EL 1410)

2. Residents participate in community activities in the area (e.g., neighborhood parties or events).
3. The active residents stem from all social groups of the population.
4. Residents proactively take the initiative to solve perceived problems.
5. Residents actively contribute to the planning and implementation of projects in the area.
6. Residents "adopt" projects in the area, i.e., they increasingly take more responsibility.
7. Public participation is fostered by effective activation techniques (e.g., providing information, activating surveys).
8. The opportunities for involvement of citizens and their spokesmen are sufficient (e.g., hearings, advisory boards, working groups).
9. Civic involvement in the area is accepted and appreciated.

B: Local Leadership

10. Individuals from the relevant offices and institutions (kindergarten, community work etc.) support the development of the area.
11. Medical doctors and individuals from other health-related services are committed to the development of the area.
12. Local leaders have the abilities to promote processes of change.
13. Local leaders motivate the area's residents to implement their ideas and projects.
14. Leadership of local stakeholders is democratic and integrative.
15. Activities in the area are documented regularly (e.g., in form of an annual report).
16. Target achievement of activities in the area is reviewed systematically.
17. Activities are adapted to local conditions (e.g., focusing on specific target groups).
18. Local leaders organize necessary qualification and training offers.

C: Available Resources

19. Funding of various projects in the area is sufficient.
20. The living environment in the area (e.g., green and playing areas, public places) meets the residents` needs.

21. The buildings in the area are in a good condition.
22. There are enough information and analyses about the area (e.g., about health and social aspects).
23. Different media (e.g., advertising paper, newspaper, internet, etc.) are used to disseminate information on area-related activities and offers.
24. Information on area-related activities and offers are conveyed to the residents in different languages.
25. The residents of the area are reached by the information media used.
26. The residents of the area know their neighbors and aid one another.
27. The residents like living in the area.
28. The residents\` needs (e.g., conviviality, celebrations) can be satisfied in the area.
29. People, who do not live here, have a good image of the area.

D: Networking and Cooperation

30. Local players (i.e., persons and/or institutions working for the area) form alliances and partnerships.
31. Relevant offices and authorities cooperate with local alliances.
32. Networks and cooperation between local players are stable.
33. Local players of the alliances in the area cooperate with other players of the city or borough.
34. There is a translocal exchange and comparison of experiences between local players in the area and other players (e.g., symposium, networks).
35. Translocal networking and cooperation between different players is stable.
36. Local cooperation partners use available information in order to overcome problems or to release potential.
37. Local partners possess the necessary competence for cooperation (e.g., communication skills, ability to resolve conflicts).
38. Local cooperating partners work together efficiently and target-oriented.
39. Local cooperating partners are perceived positively in public/in the media.

E: Health Care

40. Medical care for residents (e.g., number of general practitioners, pediatrics, gynecologists and dentists) is adequate.
41. Other health services (e.g., midwives, physiotherapy) offer sufficient health promotion.
42. The health authority and other public administration departments offer sufficient health promotion services (e.g., vaccination days, dental hygiene training).
43. Social services and educational institutions (e.g., kindergarten, schools) provide sufficient health promotion services.
44. The area`s residents are sufficiently informed about healthcare offers (e.g., general practitioners, pediatrics, gynecologists and dentists).
45. The area`s residents are sufficiently informed about health promotion services of other health services, the health authority as well as social services and educational institutions.
46. "Bridging structures" (e.g., neighborhood office, counseling or information centers) promote the use of medical practices and other healthcare facilities.
47. Medical practices and other healthcare services try to remove language and cultural barriers.
48. There are sufficient offers promoting and protecting the health of children and adolescents.
49. There are sufficient offers promoting and protecting the health of women.
50. There are sufficient offers promoting and protecting the health of men.
51. There are sufficient offers promoting and protecting the health of people with migrant backgrounds.

REFERENCES

Bortz, J., and Döring, N. (2006). Forschungsmethoden und Evaluation für Human- und Sozialwissenschaftler. 4. ed. Berlin, Heidelberg: Springer.

Bush, R., Dower, J., and Mutch, A. (2002). Community capacity index, version 2. Brisbane: University of Queensland (Centre for Primary Health Care).

Goodman, R.M., Speers, M.A., McLeroy, K., Fawcett, S., Kegler, M., Parker, E., Smith, S.R., Sterling, T.D., and Wallerstein, N. (1998). Identifying and defining the dimensions of community capacity to provide a basis for measurement. *Health Educational and Behavior,* 25 (3), 258-278.

Hawe, P., King, L., Noort, M., Jordens, C., and Lloyd, B. (2000). Indicators to help with capacity building in health promotion. Sidney: NSW Health.

Israel, B.A., Schulz, A.J., Parker, E.A., and Becker, A.B. (1998). Review of community-based research: Assessing partnership approaches to improve public health. *Annual Review of Public Health,* 19, 173-202.

Jackson, T., Mitchell, S., and Wright, M. (1989). The community development continuum. *Community Health Studies,* 13 (1), 66-73.

Kwan, B., Frankish, J., Quantz, D., and Flores, J. (2003). A synthesis paper on the conceptualization and measurement of community capacity. Vancouver: Institute of Health Promotion Research, UBC.

Labonte, R. (1990). Empowerment: Notes on professional and community dimensions. *Canadian Review of Social Policy,* 26, 64-75.

Labonte, R., and Laverack, G. (2001a). Capacity building in health promotion, part 1: For whom? And for what purpose? *Critical Public Health,* 11 (2), 111-127.

Labonte, R., and Laverack, G. (2001b). Capacity building in health promotion, part 2: Whose use? And with what measurement? *Critical Public Health,* 11 (2), 129-138.

Laverack, G. (2008). Berücksichtigung des Empowerments in der Programmplanung von Gesundheitsförderung. *Das Gesundheitswesen,* 70 (12), 736-741.

Laverack, G., and Labonte, R. (2000). A planning framework for community empowerment goals within health promotion. *Health Policy and Planning,* 15 (3), 255-262.

Liberato, S.C., Brimblecombe, J., Ritchie, J., Ferguson, M., and Coveney, J. (2011). Measuring capacity building in communities: A review of the literature. *BMC Public Health,* 11, 850.

Lienert, G.A., and Raatz, U. (1998). Testaufbau und Testanalyse. 4th. Ed. Weinheim: Psychologie-Verlags-Union.

Lorentz, C., and Trojan, A. (2013). Präventionsprogramm Lenzgesund. Das vorläufige Präventionsprogramm und seine Umsetzung. In A. Trojan, W. Süß, C. Lorentz, S. Nickel and K. Wolf (Eds.), Quartiersbezogene Gesundheitsförderung. Umsetzung und Evaluation eines integrierten lebensweltbezogenen Handlungsansatzes (pp. 65-101). Weinheim/Basel: Beltz Juventa.

Maton, K.I., and Salem, D.A. (1995). Organizational characteristics of empowering community settings: A multiple case study approach. *American Journal of Community Psychology,* 23 (5), 631-657.

Mayer, S.E. (1996). Building community capacity with evaluation activities that empower. In D.M. Fetterman, S.J. Kaftarian, and A. Wandersman (Eds.), Empowerment evaluation. Knowledge and tools for self-assessement and accountability (pp. 332-378). Thousand Oaks: Sage.

Minkler, M., and Wallerstein, N. (1997). Improving health through community organisation and community building. In K Glanz et al. (Eds.), Health behaviour and health education: Theory, research and practice (pp. 30-48). San Francisco: Jossey-Bass.

Mossakowski, K., Nickel, S., Schäfer, I., Süß, W., and Werner, S. (2007). Die Quartiersdiagnose: Daten und Ansätze für ein stadtteilorientiertes Präventionsprogramm des Öffentlichen Gesundheitsdienstes – erste Ergebnisse eines Forschungsprojektes. *Prävention und Gesundheits-förderung*, 1 (2), 82-89.

Mossakowski, K., Nickel, S., Schäfer, I., Süß, W., Trojan, A., and Werner, S. (2006). Quartiersdiagnose Lenzgesund – mehr Gesundheit ins Quartier! Daten und Ansätze zur Gesundheitsförderung in der Lenzsiedlung in Hamburg-Eimsbüttel. Hamburg.

Nickel, S., and Trojan, A. (2013a). Kapazitätsentwicklung im Quartier am Beispiel der Lenzsiedlung. In A. Trojan, W. Süß, C. Lorentz, S. Nickel and K. Wolf (Eds.), Quartiersbezogene Gesundheitsförderung. Umsetzung und Evaluation eines integrierten lebensweltbezogenen Handlungsansatzes (pp. 240-246). Weinheim/Basel: Beltz Juventa.

Nickel, S., and Trojan, A. (2013b). KEQ-Transfertests in fünf anderen Gebieten. In A. Trojan, W. Süß, C. Lorentz, S. Nickel and K. Wolf (Eds.), Quartiersbezogene Gesundheitsförderung. Umsetzung und Evaluation eines integrierten lebensweltbezogenen Handlungsansatzes (pp. 247-256). Weinheim/Basel: Beltz Juventa.

Nickel, S., and Trojan, A. (2009). Zur Messung von Kapazitätsentwicklung im Quartier: Konzept, Methode, Erfahrungen. In P. Kolip and V. Müller (Eds.), Qualität von Gesundheitsförderung und Prävention. Handbuch Gesundheitswissenschaften (pp. 279-293). Bern: Verlag Hans Huber.

Noack, H., and Reis-Klingspiegl, K. (2006). Building health promotion capacities in local settings: Community readiness and community participation. In H. Noack and D. Kahr-Gottlieb (Eds.), Promoting the public's health. EUPHA 2005 Conference Book (pp. 113-122). Gamburg: Verlag für Gesundheitsförderung.

Nutbeam, D. (1998). Evaluating health promotion – progress, problems and solutions. *Health Promotion International,* 13 (1), 27-44.

Ogilvie, D., Cummins, S., Petticrew, M., White, M., Jones, A., and Wheeler, K. (2011). Assessing the evaluability of complex public health interventions: Five questions for researchers, funders, and policymakers. *Milbank Quarterly,* 89 (2), 206-225.

Raithel, J. (2008). Quantitative Forschung. Ein Praxiskurs. Wiesbaden: VS Verlag.

Rifkin, S. (2003). A framework linking community empowerment and health equity: It is a matter of CHOICE. *Journal of Health, Population, and Nutrition,* 21 (3), 168-180.

Schnell, R., Hill, P.B., and Esser, E. (1993). Methoden der empirischen Sozialforschung. 4. Ed. München: R. Oldenbourg.

Stockmann, R. (2000). Evaluation in Deutschland. In R. Stockmann (Ed.), Evaluationsforschung. Grundlagen und ausgewählte Forschungsfelder (pp. 11-40). Opladen: Leske and Budrich Verlag.

Trojan, A., and Nickel, S. (2013). Konzept und Methode des Instruments zur Messung der Kapazitätsentwicklung. In A. Trojan, W. Süß, C. Lorentz, S. Nickel and K. Wolf (Eds.), Quartiersbezogene Gesundheitsförderung. Umsetzung und Evaluation eines integrierten lebensweltbezogenen Handlungsansatzes (pp. 218-227). Weinheim/Basel: Beltz Juventa.

Walter, U., and Schwartz, F.W. (2003). Prävention. In F.W. Schwartz (Ed.), Das Public Health Buch. Gesundheit und Gesundheitswesen (pp. 189-191). München und Jena: Urban and Fischer.

WHO – World Health Organization (Ed.) (2009). Milestones in health üromotion. Statements from global conferences. Geneva: World Health Organization.

In: Capacity Building
Editor: Diane Brown

ISBN: 978-1-63483-995-2

Chapter 5

BUILDING CAPACITY TO ADAPT TO THE CONSEQUENCES OF DISASTER: LINKING DISASTER RECOVERY AND DISASTER RISK REDUCTION

Douglas Paton*[1]*, PhD, Li-ju Jang*[2]*, PhD and Melanie Irons*[3]*, PhD

[1]School of Psychological and Clinical Sciences, Charles Darwin University, Darwin, Northern Territory, Australia
[2]Department of Social Work, National Pingtung University of Science and Technology, Pingtung, Taiwan, ROC
[3]School of Psychology, University of Tasmania, Hobart, Tasmania, Australia

ABSTRACT

In locations that expose citizens to large scale disasters, a key disaster risk reduction (DRR) goal is developing their adaptive capacity. The atypical nature of disasters make it important to understand how people, individually and collectively, adapt when experiencing disaster. This chapter discusses research on disaster recovery in New Zealand (2011 Christchurch earthquake), Taiwan (1999 Chi Chi earthquake) and Australia (2013 Tasmanian wildfire) and the lessons learnt regarding how personal, family, community and societal factors interact to facilitate adaptation to the consequences of disaster.

Data from the 2011 Christchurch earthquake and 1999 Chi Chi earthquake were obtained as survivors confronted the demands of disaster recovery. By collecting data from the 2013 Tasmanian wildfire using a Facebook page (Tassie Fires – We Can Help) specifically developed to assess response and recovery, the chapter offers rare in situ, real-time insights into adaptive demands and adaptive responses. These analyses are used to provide insights into adaption, and how models and theories of capacity building can be developed from such experience to inform the planning and design of capacity building programs. By conducting this work in countries that differ extensively in their cultural characteristics (comparing Taiwan and Australia/New Zealand), the chapter affords an opportunity to develop understanding of how cultural similarities and differences inform how capacity is developed, sustained and enacted.

INTRODUCTION

When hazard events occur, citizens in affected areas are suddenly confronted with losses, disruptions and demands that differ significantly from what they are likely to experience in everyday life. People need to adapt to these demands and they need to do so in circumstances often characterized by little, and sometimes no, support from normal societal resources, functions and activities (e.g., transportation, water and power services, employment etc.). Consequently, adaptation centres on people's ability, both individually and collectively, to respond using their own resources and capabilities and/or by being able to work with external agencies (government, non-government organisations (NGOs), and businesses) to facilitate their own recovery.

Analyses of people's disaster experiences make it clear that people and communities differ with regard to how well they adapt to these conditions. Some adapt well, others less so, while some need considerable assistance. The evident diversity in how people adapt provides a context that affords opportunities to develop understanding of why people and communities vary in their capacities to adapt to hazard-related losses and disruption (Bruijn, 2004; Carpenter et al. 2001; Gaillard, 2007; Klein, Nicholls, and Thomalla, 2003; Norris et al. 2008; Paton, 2006a,b; Pelling and High, 2005). Furthermore, if the reasons for such differences can be articulated, this knowledge can be used to inform how the goal of linking disaster and development (the Build Back Better philosophy) emphasized in the Sendai Framework (United Nations, 2015) can be actively pursued in contemporary disaster risk reduction (DRR) initiatives. Doing so contributes to facilitating how the phoenix of resilience (Paton and Gow, 2008) can rise from the disaster and contribute to the development of future, sustainable person, household, community and societal adaptive capabilities.

This chapter contributes to understanding how this can be done by drawing on research conducted during the response and recovery phases of three disasters; the 1999 Chi Chi (921) earthquake in Taiwan, the 2011 Christchurch (New Zealand) earthquake, and the 2013 Tasmanian (Australia) bushfire (wildfire) (Irons, 2015; Jang, 2008; Paton and Jang, 2013; Paton, Johnston, Mamula-Seadon and Kenney, 2014). Conducting research at a time when people are embedded in their recovery makes it possible to gain valuable insights into what they experienced, what they need to adapt to, and the psychological, social and societal factors that contributed to how well they were able to adapt.

The first issue to be considered is identifying the adaptive challenges or demands that disasters present to those affected. Once these are articulated, the focus can then turn to identifying the factors that influence how well people deal with them. The events selected for discussion in this chapter presented those affected with a range of issues to confront and adapt to.

WHAT DO PEOPLE NEED TO ADAPT TO?

The 2011, MW 6.3 earthquake that struck Christchurch resulted in 85 deaths, damaged some 100,000 homes, rendered about 7,000 uninhabitable, resulted in over 7000 injuries, and caused more than US$12 billion in damage (Bannister and Gledhill, 2012). The second event discussed in this chapter, the MW 7.6 921 (Chi Chi) earthquake in central Taiwan in 1999 caused 2,415 deaths, 11,306 injuries, rendered some 114,000 homes uninhabitable, damaged 1500 schools, and made some 110,000 people homeless (Lin, 2002; Lo, 2010). The third event, the 2013 Tasmanian wildfire, did not result in loss of life, but as the ensuing State government-commissioned Bushfire Inquiry noted, the event created significant physical, economic, social, psychological and environmental damage (DPAC, 2013). Overall, some 431 properties were damaged or destroyed, including 203 residential buildings. The impact on the rural community was substantial and losses were estimated at more than $100 million.

The data on which the discussion in this chapter is based were obtained from interviews with survivors in Christchurch and in Tung Shia and via the analysis of Facebook posts in Tasmania (Irons, 2015; Jang, 2008; Paton et al.

2014). The interviews in Christchurch and Tung Shia were conducted during the period of recovery. By using Facebook data obtained from a specifically developed Facebook page, the Tassie Fires - We Can Help (TFWCH) page afforded opportunities to gain firsthand insights into what people were experiencing and what they were doing to adapt during the response phase. This work thus provided a unique window into disaster experience and response as they unfolded in real time.

The first issue discussed concerns people's accounts of what they encountered and experienced and thus what people need to adapt to. The adaptive demands and the adaptive competencies that contributed to adaptation in Christchurch are summarized in Figure 1. The contents of Figure 1 illustrate how adaptive demands changed over time as people progressively dealt with impact, response and recovery demands. Figure 1 also illustrates how adaptive capacities reflect the interdependent influence of person, family, community and societal factors. The relative contributions of each of these levels of analysis to the response to the adaptive demands are presented in Figure 1 as dotted lines.

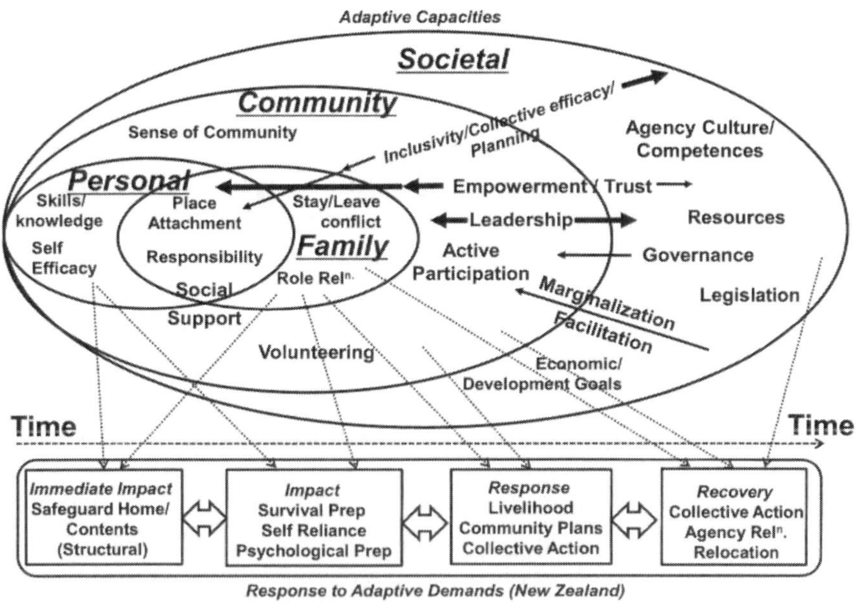

Figure 1. A summary of the interdependent influence of person, family, community and societal adaptive capacities on individual and collective response to adaptive demands experienced following the 2011 Christchurch earthquake.

ADAPTIVE DEMANDS

New Zealand

Interviews with Christchurch residents (Paton et al. 2014) during the ongoing aftershock sequence asked residents about the direct (e.g., issues arising from ground shaking, liquefaction etc.) and indirect (e.g., loss of infrastructure, amenities etc.) demands and challenges they had to adapt to. The direct impact of the earthquakes created demands from damage to homes and infrastructure. This experience resulted in respondents recognizing inadequacies in their structural readiness (e.g., problems linked to their not having secured the house to its foundations, or strapped chimneys to prevent their collapse).

The lack of these structural readiness measures reduced the level of survivability of and physical protection offered by the home when impacted by hazard effects. Respondents also discussed how the loss of infrastructure and services created adaptive demands that could have been responded to by, for example, storing emergency supplies of food and water and planning how the family would be self-reliant during this time (Figure 1).

The lack of structural preparedness was identified as increasing the adaptive demands people faced (e.g., having to move out of the home). Respondents reported how their lack of such readiness and planning made adjusting to the loss of water, power and sewerage services more challenging than it needed to be. Not only did this reduce their capacity for self-reliance, it meant diverting precious time and energy to accessing essentials like water and temporary toilet facilities rather than attending to family needs and planning how best to respond to their circumstances (e.g., dealing with employment issues). Respondents also identified challenges arising from constantly having to cope with their own and family members' stress, having to adapt to changes in living conditions, loss of social relationships and livelihood disruptions throughout the several months over which recovery took place (Figure 1).

This discussion illustrates how adaptation is facilitated when a person prepares their home and their immediate neighbourhood, and plans how they will deal with a wide range of demands, such as the need to be self-reliant in meeting both physical and psychological needs. These activities make additional secondary contributions to personal, community and societal adaptation.

Being able to remain in a habitable home increases people's availability within a neighborhood to offer mutual assistance and social support to others and to be available to contribute to economic recovery (as customers and employees).

A need to adapt to hazard consequences was not restricted to the period of impact alone (Figure 1). Adaptive demands changed as people transitioned through the recovery and reconstruction phases. Christchurch residents discussed how the recovery phase included their having to develop ways of responding to the loss and damage in their neighbourhood. People discussed how being able to work with neighbors and other community members to develop (self-help) groups to confront local demands (e.g., removing rubble, proving mutual support, setting up community meeting places, taking care of those with special needs) represented important adaptive responses (Figure 1). This included either re-establishing community groups and applying collective efforts in novel ways or forming new ones to provide a basis for meeting local recovery needs (e.g., organizing local efforts to repair homes, identifying and meeting local needs). It quickly became clear that community members did not always have the resources (e.g., knowledge, skills, equipment) to meet their own needs.

As societal recovery processes became more established, respondents discussed how community members' ability to identify their own recovery needs and to be able to represent their needs to agencies (e.g., government, businesses, NGOs etc.) became an adaptive demand (Figure 1).

The quality of people's relationship with agency sources played a key role in their ability to secure the resources they needed to allow them to continue to take responsibility for their own recovery. Thus, it was evident that what people had to contend with changed over time (e.g., from loss of utilities, to making neighborhoods safe, to dealing with government agencies) as they negotiated physical, social and institutional demands that altered over the course of a prolonged period of recovery.

Similar issues to those discussed above emerged in the analysis of recovery from the second event discussed here, the 1999, 921 or Chi Chi earthquake in Taiwan (Jang, 2008). The examples discussed below come from data collected from Tung Shia in central Taiwan. The adaptive demands and associated capacities that emerged here are summarized in Figure 2.

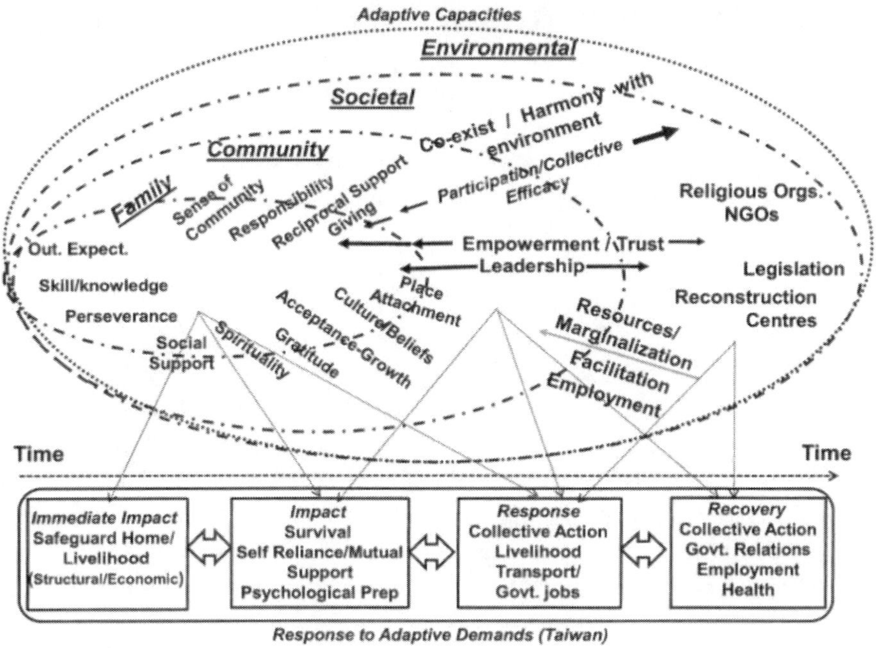

Figure 2. A summary of the interdependent influence of person, family, community and societal adaptive capacities on individual and collective response to adaptive demands experienced following the 1999, 921 earthquake in Taiwan.

Taiwan

In Taiwan (Jang, 2008) discernible similarities with New Zealand were evident regarding the adaptive demands Tung Shia residents discussed. There were also differences. Tung Shia residents identified physical loss and damage, the need to have the resources to be self-reliant during periods of maximum disruption, and the importance of anticipating (planning) what and for how long disruption and deprivation would persist as significant adaptive demands. Compared with New Zealand, Tung Shia residents afforded livelihood issues the same level of priority as they did structural demands (Figure 2). This reflects the affected area being an agricultural one, with demands on livelihood arising from damage and infrastructure losses affecting, for example, not being able to get fresh produce to markets.

Overall, as in New Zealand, residents identified the important role that structural (e.g., building code reinforcement, home safety), survival (e.g., resource availability, food/water storage, personal safety) and planning (e.g., getting produce to markets) readiness played in facilitating their ability to adapt to hazard consequences. Taiwanese respondents also identified the role hazard knowledge played in helping people to be able to quickly and calmly cope with the psychological correlates of the demands experienced. In doing so, they identified how the psychological impact of a disaster represented a significant adaptive demand (Figure 2).

Taiwanese respondents' accounts echoed their NZ counterparts regarding the need for community members to take responsibility for such things as local repairs and ensuring that the needs of more vulnerable members of the community could be met by themselves (Figure 2). Similar to what was found in New Zealand, Taiwanese respondents acknowledged that while community self-reliance was important, the atypical and severe nature of the impacts meant that some measure of societal support was essential (e.g., to assist infrastructure repair, provide temporary income or provide alternative ways of getting produce to markets). It was also evident, in both New Zealand and Taiwan that some people and groups were able to adapt to these atypical circumstances better than others.

ACCOUNTING FOR DIFFERENCES IN PEOPLE'S ADAPTIVE CAPACITY

Respondents in both New Zealand and Taiwan faced comparable adaptive demands (Figures 1 and 2). Differences were also evident in each location with regard how people, individually and collectively, dealt with recovery demands. Some did better than others. The existence of such differences provides an opportunity to explore how their respective community capacities and characteristics can account for these differences in levels of adaptation.

The in-depth interviews identified several factors that offered insights into the personal, community and societal factors that influenced how people responded to these adaptive demands. These are summarized in Figures 1 and 2 for New Zealand and Taiwan respectively. It is to these that the discussion now turns, starting with the individual, family, community and societal factors that emerged in the Christchurch analysis (Figure1).

New Zealand

Individual and Family-Level Influences on Adaptation

While unable to (retrospectively) do anything about the recognized deficiencies in structural readiness, participants acknowledged the crucial role structural readiness plays in adaptation (Paton et al. 2014). Respondents speculated that having relevant knowledge and skills and having a 'mind-set' of getting the job done (cf. self-efficacy) would be important precursors of structural readiness. They also suggested that place attachment and a sense of both personal and social responsibility (see also McIvor, Paton and Johnston, 2009) for household and neighbourhood safety could influence structural readiness (e.g., the stronger the feeling of attachment to place, the more likely they would be to protect their home) and the degree to which they would work with neighbors to confront local issues. The effectiveness of people's recovery was also influenced by family factors (Figure 1).

Some respondents reflected on how family circumstances affected their commitment to structural and planning readiness. Family disagreement, particularly if the male member of the household was opposed to work in this area, could affect role relationships within a family and result in readiness and planning being seen as unimportant. During the response, family disagreement about whether to stay or to leave influenced whether they would get involved in local community-based activities. This had a secondary consequence in that it reduced opportunities for access to social support.

Community-Level Influences on Adaptation

Engaging with others and maintaining relationships emerged as important influences on adaptation (Mamula-Seadon, Paton and Selway, 2012; Paton et al. 2014). Maintaining active relationships contributed to people being able to develop a sense of belonging and identity that served to create feelings of connectedness to people and place and generated a sense of commitment to the recovery. Sense of community was also identified as arising not just from sharing the same fate as others, but from having to work with them to effectively confront and resolve local issues over time (Figure 1).

Being able to collaborate to confront local issues laid a strong foundation for collective efficacy and planning. One focus group discussed how having to fend for themselves during the early stages of the response phase led to their developing collaborative efforts with neighbours that were sustained over several months. The level of active participation in neighbourhood activities, and the degree to which local networks sought to include as many people as possible (inclusivity) became key adaptive capacities and influenced people's ability to meet local needs and obtain social support from a broader social network (Figure 1). Access to a broader network also increased the available knowledge and skill base and thus the collective capacity for planning and action. This highlights the importance of collective efficacy as a predictor of adaptation, and one that plays an important role in facilitating community members' capacity to take responsibility for their own recovery.

Focus group data (Paton, 2012) identified other important predictors of effective recovery. For example, community members who were proactive and willing to take action to deal with emergent needs even when operating under conditions of scarce or unreliable information; and who made efforts to involve others (inclusivity) in, for example, problem prioritization and collective planning contributed positively to recovery. This, in turn, was seen as an important aspect of community empowerment. This capacity was further bolstered by the level of local leadership.

A community resource that was pivotal to effective community response was community leaders. Emergent leaders brought people together, facilitated the development and implementation of activities around salient community issues, and linked the community with external agencies and specialists to secure the resources and help required to meet local community needs (Paton, et al. 2014). Effective community leaders were characterized by a number of key factors: a strong commitment to helping others; an understanding of what went on in their community and how to get people to work together, practical experience in leadership roles, the ability to take action in uncertain and challenging circumstances, and knowing who and how to call on government and business to assist their community (Mamula-Seadon et al. 2012).

The last point reiterates how, in complex disaster recovery environments, communities also need information and resources that must be sourced from, for example, government agencies, NGOs and businesses. It is, however, important to appreciate that the ability of agencies to facilitate adaptation involves more than their being able to provide resources. The quality of the community-agency relationship is also important, and is affected by factors such as governance processes, agency crisis management procedures and agency culture and staff training (Figure 1).

Community-Agency/Government Relationship-Level Influences on Adaptation

Positive community-agency relationships in Christchurch were facilitated by government and relief agencies using community leaders as the conduit into communities. This increased the likelihood that agency-sourced information and resources complemented community activities. Governance solutions emerged through the establishment of dedicated local recovery organizations (e.g., CERA, CanCERN) (Mamula-Seadon et al. 2012).

However, marginalization was also evident from focus group participants describing the government emergency response as often poorly coordinated, lacking local contacts, and not knowing of local distribution locations (Paton, 2012). For example, welfare and social services agencies and staff were perceived to be working in isolation (the often-lamented 'silo effect') with little coordination of functions, thereby reducing their capacity to empower community initiatives. Problems were compounded by the fact that these agencies were operating from locations several hundred kilometres removed from the disaster. They thus had little clear idea of what people were experiencing and the constraints on what people could do and they lacked the crisis response training required to adapt to the changed conditions and needs of those in disaster-affected areas. Thus the relationship between government agencies and businesses and communities can facilitate or marginalize community recovery (Figure 1).

Community-agency relationships that acted to disempower or marginalize community members had knock-on effects in that they reduced trust in agencies and thus the quality of future relationships. A loss of trust early in the recovery reduced the capacity of agency sources to assist recovery. Taken together, this discussion identifies adaptation as a multi-level phenomenon in which people, communities and agencies must play complementary roles (Figure 1). This notion of 'shared responsibility' is a gold standard, but very challenging to achieve. The importance of appreciating this was reinforced by the Taiwan study.

Taiwan

The Taiwanese data were obtained from Hakka residents in Tung Shih, Taiwan. The Hakka people form the second largest ethnic group in Taiwan and comprise some 20% of the population. A unique aspect of Hakka life revolves round the Hakka Spirit, the essence of Hakka culture. The Hakka Spirit comprises characteristics such as frugality, diligence, self-reliance, shared responsibility, and persistence (Yang, 2004). This is introduced here as the Hakka Spirit was linked to their recovery. While elements of the Hakka Spirit are comparable to the constructs that emerged in the Christchurch analysis, the difference is that, in Taiwan, they are culturally implicit and more readily available. The Hakka Spirit was implicated in generating a sustained sense of purpose and perseverance (which creates a kind of culture-specific self-efficacy) despite hardships and assisted people's efforts to re-build their homes and communities (Jang, 2008). Key findings are summarized in Figure 2.

Individual-Level Influences on Adaptation

In Taiwan, after witnessing the level of destruction from the 921 earthquake, some participants expressed the belief that earthquake consequences were too catastrophic for personal action to make any difference (i.e., negative outcome expectancy) to peoples' safety (Jang, 2008; Paton and Jang, 2011). However, a characteristic comparable to positive outcome expectancy was also discernible in people's accounts, and one that reflects Hakka people's history of dealing hazard consequences. Jang and LaMendola (2006) discussed how farming practices that evolved to limit the impact of typhoons on people's livelihoods generated enduring outcome expectancy beliefs (Figure 2). That is, a culturally embedded belief in the ability of collective actions to overcome challenges carried over into people's beliefs regarding their ability to adapt to the novel circumstances created by the disaster.

As with their New Zealand counterparts, Taiwanese respondents commented on the importance of hazard knowledge and skills. Participants emphasized that being self-reliant made them feel happy and fuelled their sense of achievement in how they adapted to the circumstances they encountered. This was further reinforced by their sense of perseverance and a belief that irrespective of how hard one is tested by a disaster life must go on. These cultural characteristics, in turn, underpinned people's belief in the importance of being proactive and not 'just waiting' for assistance from government or NGOs to arrive. Thus, as in New Zealand, being proactive under conditions of uncertainty is an important predictor of adaptation.

An interesting addition to adaptive resources derived from Hakka beliefs regards the importance of learning to accept disasters as part of life experience and of living and co-existing harmoniously with nature (Figure 2). Both characteristics had positive impacts on people's response to the 921 earthquake (Jang, 2008; Jang and LaMendola, 2006). Participants discussed how they likened natural disasters to ordeals from Heaven: because they cannot change what has happened, they accept what has happened and focus on dealing with the present. This represents a kind of spiritually-sourced, cultural problem-focused coping that assisted their adaptive recovery (Jang, 2008). Spirituality was influential in other ways.

Spirituality offers explanations for death, life, loss, and natural disasters and helps survivors identify inner strengths and find meaning in people's sufferings and behaviours. In Taiwan, participants indicated that religious beliefs helped them cope with challenges, be more optimistic, and to see the positive aspects of their experience (e.g., people pulling together to promote the recovery of the whole community). Participants discussed how religious beliefs encouraged people to work on personal merits and practice moral culture. This reflects how spirituality in Taiwan is a way of life, and one that promotes positive interpretations of challenging experiences (Jang and LaMendola, 2007). Spirituality also supported people's sense of community, and strengthened their social support networks.

Family and Community-Level Influences on Adaptation

For the Hakka survivors of the 921 earthquake, their social support networks were pivotal in helping them adapt. People's social support networks not only provided a mechanism for managing psychological issues, it also served as a context in which people could serve others (Figure 2). This, in turn, contributed to making people feel needed, wanted and belonging (cf. sense of community). The process of serving others both contributed to being able to offer meaningful help to others and assisted survivors themselves to grow. This culturally inherent reciprocal helping contributed to survivors gaining new meaning and explanation for life after disasters (see also Farley 1998). An essential source of social support networks came from family. Participants with a sense of responsibility toward their families and communities were more likely to apply a problem-focused coping style to their recovery efforts (Jang, 2008).

Taiwanese respondents also endorsed the key role of community processes and community leadership as drivers of effective recovery. Community leaders were described in terms of their ability to understand local needs and priorities and for their role in local response planning and emergency operations (Jang and LaMendola, 2006). Tung Shia residents discussed how they believe that they are experts on their community concerns and problems and that practical and coping resources should be developed by them to meet local needs. This did not mean that external agencies played no role in adaptation. Respondents acknowledged the need for external experts under the extraordinary circumstances created by the disaster. Respondents discussed the need for agency activity to complement and empower community activities (e.g., as technical assistants, information providers, and resource brokers) rather than supplanting them (Jang, 2008).

Community-Agency/Government Relationship-Level Influences on Adaptation

As was the case in New Zealand, the ability of agencies (e.g., government, NGOs) to support community adaptation extended beyond just making resources available. As in New Zealand, government actions could facilitate or marginalize community members. For example, the Taiwanese Government created temporary positions for survivors. However, access to this potentially adaptive resource was seldom available to those who would most benefit; it was people with connections with local government that took those positions (Jang, 2008). Regardless, facilitation and empowerment was evident in relationships with other agencies. Temporary housing (prefabs) was built by religious groups (in Taiwan, religious groups are major sources of community services) and NGOs to provide shelters for survivors. A measure of empowerment was built into this process by their actively including survivors in reconstruction projects (e.g., being involved in designing and (re)building their own houses). Facilitation was also evident in the Government providing free loans to assist these rebuilding efforts. Developing relationships through joint ventures with local people, local government, farmers associations and other occupational associations, non-profit organizations, and religious groups were identified as playing key roles in creating community-agency relationships that fostered adaptation.

Australia

The above analyses, while conducted during the period of recovery and reconstruction, involved some degree of retrospective analysis. The third study discussed in this chapter involved the analysis of social media posts when people were in the response environment. This afforded opportunity to explore people's experiences, needs, goals, problems and responses in situ and in real time. This third analysis can thus provide insights that can validate and expand on the analysis of adaptive needs and processes in disaster contexts. This analysis (Irons, 2015) provides insights into what people encountered and the personal and collective processes people drew on to facilitate their adaptation using data obtained via the development of a Facebook page (Tassie Fires - We Can Help – TFWCH) specifically set up to facilitate disaster response.

The first issue discussed relates to the demands people experienced and the resources they identified as essential to their adaptive efforts. People's ability to adapt and respond (rather than react) is fundamentally a function of the timely availability of relevant, robust, redundant and useable (from a community perspective) resources (Norris et al. 2008). In New Zealand and Taiwan, significant issues arose from people's need to secure the resources they needed in situ. The Australian study illustrated how social media could expedite the sharing and exchange of relevant and meaningful information and resources in a timely (rapid) manner.

In a disaster, people turn to social media to get help (Blanchard, Carvin, Whittaker, Fitzgerald, Harman and Humphrey, 2010). A key way in which online emergent groups can facilitate adaptation is via rapid communication and information exchange (Vieweg et al. 2010). This enhances the capacity of people and communities to respond quickly to changes in conditions (a hallmark of disasters, which are fluid and ambiguous events), often within a matter of minutes.

Social media offers robustness and redundancy within this process, both issues described by Norris et al. (2008) as important for adaptation. Social media creates a large information and resource "crowd" and the diversity of the resources that are implicit within this crowd increases the speed with which people can access resources that are relevant to their needs at the time they are needed. In the absence of such an online emergent group, organizing to meet diverse community needs is very difficult, if not impossible. Compared with their formal response counterparts (e.g, Fire and Emergency Services), online emergent groups facilitate adaptation as a result of their capacity to source and transfer the specific resources that survivor groups need in timely ways. They also offer resource redundancy.

Redundancy increases the likelihood that if a group cannot access resources from one quarter, others may be able to step in. Online emergent groups not only increase the number of accessible sources able to contribute, but because these resources are geographically distributed, they offer redundancy and robustness. In the Australian wildfire case study, redundancy is apparent in that many different people were engaging in a variety of volunteering activities (Irons, 2015). This last point, volunteering, has additional adaptive implications by increasing the scope and capacity of "community," via networked relationships that people in affected areas can draw on. The importance of the latter was highlighted in Christchurch where the novel nature of the demands encountered required the development of new relationships and networks with others in their neighborhoods. A similar process was evident in Australia, but this process, and its inherent capabilities, was heightened by the development of relationships via social media and the emergent development of social capital that could be readily and rapidly invested in community adaptation and recovery.

Social Capital

Norris et al. (2008) discussed how interconnectedness between people is pivotal to their accessing social support, feeling a sense of belonging or community, and being attached to place, with these representing important adaptive resources in post-disaster recovery. The TFWCH resource enabled those impacted to develop new networks in the context of their disaster experience with people, groups and agencies ('strangers' were helping 'strangers') with whom they were unlikely to have contact with outside of the disaster context. Furthermore, it would have been impossible to have developed these within the DRR context as the role the emergent relationships played in response was context-specific. People cannot predict what they will experience or need. This echoes some of the adaptive challenges experienced in New Zealand and Taiwan. The novelty of the circumstances and issues people encountered involved the rapid emergence of new physical relationships and/or called for existing relationships to develop new ways of working (Jang, 2008; Paton et al. 2014).

Online emergent groups act as a resource that can furnish expertise and information in rapid and relevant ways to deal with emergent, evolving issues. This reiterates the view that resilience and adaptive capacity must be conceptualized in context (Bruijn, 2004; Carpenter et al. 2001; Gaillard, 2007; Klein et al. Norris et al. 2008; Paton, 2006; Pelling and High, 2005). Social networking sites can also facilitate the development and application of local networks as they can facilitate resident-to-resident communication and interaction.

The sense of community and affiliation that arise via social media (Beyerlein and Sikkink, 2008) can not only increase the opportunities for volunteering to occur, but also expedite the process of ensuring that volunteers complement community activities and needs (Irons, 2015). Having a central hub such as TFWCH helped people to feel connected with the survivors as they heard and shared their stories, with this consolidating their sense of community. Attachment to place is another aspect of social capital that has been implicated in adaptation (Norris et al. 2008).

While an online emergent group may not be able to increase attachment to place during a crisis, it may be able to allow members of a community with a strong attachment to place to more readily translate this into meaningful action. Hence, online emergent groups, such as TFWCH, can mobilize the kinds of adaptive resources (e.g., sense of community, social support, place attachment etc.) that are cited as important in disaster recovery (Jang, 2008; Paton et al. 2014).

The New Zealand and Taiwan analyses identified pivotal roles for empowerment and trust, with both of these drivers of adaptation being linked to issues surrounding being able to access accurate, timely information and being able to share their experiences and understandings of an event (Paton et al. 2014). Social media can facilitate the ability of formal authorities and agencies to provide information and assistance that is tailored for specific communities and so empower community activities. A prominent strength of social media is its ability to enable information to be communicated from both the top down and from the bottom up (Belblidia, 2010). It can thus play a pivotal role in empowering response and increasing the likelihood of trusting relationships developing within the recovery environment. A key element here is the ability of social media to accommodate diversity (e.g., ethnicity, culture, age and educational level etc.) in ways that are very challenging through more conventional forms of engagement.

Under normal circumstances, it is very difficult for agencies to tailor information to meet the range of needs that emerge within the recovery space (Paton et al. 2014). Through social media resources, such as the community-based TFWCH page, community leaders and community members were able to disseminate official information when required, but also to provide specific content linked to local needs. This increased the likelihood that survivors saw formal information as accurate, trustworthy and relevant. Furthermore, the TFWCH resource was able to encourage residents to review information critically and to actively translate formal information to fit local needs. This approach illustrates how social media can act as a mechanism that can facilitate the kind of community-agency relationships identified as important for adaptation during disaster recovery (Jang, 2008; Paton et al. 2014). Social media arguably makes traditional media and responding organizations more accountable, as the general public can have a voice in the online and therefore offline space. This expedites the development of community-agency relationships (see Figures 1 and 2). With the use of social media, the general public can be more engaged in the recovery conversation, and throw light on the potential disparities between the messages that formal responders are giving, and what is really happening 'on the ground.'

Through social media, people can gather and exchange information on diverse topics (for example, how to get assistance with mental health issues, where to get financial assistance, or finding places offering child care). This represents what can be regarded as "collective intelligence" (Vieweg et al. 2008). This can map onto the collective efficacy identified in the New Zealand and Taiwan studies as playing a key role in facilitating adaptation. It does so by contributing to the development of community competence (Eng and Parker, 1994; Norris et al. 2008)

Community competency, according to the above authors, represents a suite of resources that include, for example, the encouragement of inclusivity and active involvement in social activities, the facilitation of critical problem solving, the ability to engage in collective behaviors and to engage in meaningful action, and the ability to represent community needs to the wider society. All of these emerged as antecedents of adaptation in the New Zealand and Taiwan studies, as well as in readiness research (Paton, 2008). The analysis of the functioning of the TFWCH page provided ample evidence of its capacity to facilitate and sustain these competencies (Gardner, 2013; Irons, 2015). The capacities so instilled in this emergent group laid the foundation for their empowerment.

Accessing, and being able to function through, an emergent online group facilitated people's ability to use their initiative, knowledge and connections to work independently on their response and recovery. The opportunity for the community to collaborate and engage in community action to assist their own recovery is a key component of resilience (Lowe and Fothergill, 2003; Norris et al. 2008). While offline groups and official responders could (and do) respond to evolving situations, it is argued that provided the necessary technological infrastructure is still operating, social media driven emergent groups can do it faster and more efficiently. The ability for an emergent group to evolve and improvise as the situation changes like this is a key component of their importance in a disaster situation, as they are able to respond and adapt more quickly that other organizations or agencies that must function in much more centralized ways.

Story Telling and Psychosocial Support

Another element relating to information and communication raised by Norris et al. (2008) is story-telling and sharing. Facebook facilitates story-telling and sharing, similar to "circle" processes detailed above, as people can congregate and chat using the comments function under each Facebook post. Without a key online hub for people to congregate in this is something that would not as easily occur. It is therefore argued that this social media driven emergent group contributed to the element of story-telling and sharing considerably. The Administrator was regularly sharing stories, reflecting on the successes of the emergent group, and giving progress reports. Stories can be used to facilitate the development of a Build Back Better (see below) approach to recovery by providing a context people can more readily identify with and which can be used to provide more realistic appreciation of what can be encountered and what people "like them" recommend doing to ameliorate loss and suffering. This could serve as a vehicle for increasing the likelihood of people being able to personalize issues and develop a greater appreciation of it might mean for them.

In both the New Zealand and Taiwan analyses, participants identified psychological issues as significant adaptive demands. In New Zealand, respondents believed that psychological preparedness should be given a high priority in future DRR strategies (Paton et al. 2014). The Australian population echoed the significance of psychological demands encountered during disaster response, but also introduced the potential for social media to facilitate people's ability to cope and adapt to these psychological demands (Irons, 2015; Lowe and Fothergill, 2003). This can occur in several ways. One reflects a benefit of the story-telling opportunities outlined above, and their influence on people's ability to impose meaning on their experience (Steffen and Lowe, 2009). Membership of an online emergent group can also assist in this context as a medium through which psychological first aid can be obtained.

The TFWCH page provided information about sources of psychosocial support (e.g., social workers, trauma recovery specialists). This had a secondary benefit with regard to facilitating the development of community-agency links that play key roles in adaptation (see Figures 1 and 2). However, psychological adaptation was also supported by the connections available through the page positively impacting on people's psychological states. The page assisted people to feel part of a supportive community and it connected people in similar circumstances in ways that facilitated their ability to access and provide the emotional, informational and belongingness social support that assists people to manage stress, especially when the sources of stress persist over time (Irons, 2015; Lowe and Fothergill, 2003). For example, people discussed how being able to connect with strangers through the network online to source assistance or find ways to cope was important. It was also evident that providing people with information helped them to feel calm, hopeful, connected and safe, and able to enact change themselves (Irons, 2015). Being a part of an online emergent group can facilitate the healing process, particularly when delivered within a community setting, rather than in a clinical setting (Burke et al. 2013).

Leadership

The Australian analysis furnished evidence regarding the important role community-based leadership plays in adaptation. The analysis of TFWCH reinforced the importance of the leader attribute of empathy in the functioning of an online emergent group. Leadership activities of providing clear instructions, updates, and information about how help could be offered, and actively encouraging and motivating people to do so, was highlighted. Providing opportunities for people to help (cf. Taiwan), ensuring that people felt supported and valued, acknowledging and reinforcing the value of all contributions emerged as important leadership tasks (Irons, 2015). Behling and McFillen (2006) argue that the performance of these tasks is crucial to both inspiring people and supporting empowerment.

Leadership competencies echoed those found in New Zealand and Taiwan regarding the information brokerage and management role. Crucial here was the ability to filter information against background "noise" and to be able to both identify what information is relevant for which group, to be able to mobilize the critical capacities of recipients to focus on what was relevant for them, and to use information to include others whose expertise or capabilities may be important for the issues being faced at a specific time (Behling and McFillen, 1996; Eysenbach, 2008; Irons, 2015). Leader legitimacy, particularly with regard to how leaders are regarded by others, assists leader ability to sustain community activities (Stallings and Quarantelli, 1985). This can be supported by, for example, formally voting for community leaders (Paton et al. 2014).

It is argued that the leader of an emergent online group is a critical factor in being the 'activator.' Skillful and legitimate leadership is fundamental to the online page being transformed into a viable vehicle through which the community can contribute to response and recovery, access assistance and psychological first aid, and become architects in their own resilience.

A common denominator in all three case studies was finding that, when faced with adversity, all the communities discussed evolved ways of adapting through applying pre-event social competencies in new ways or developing new ways of relating to people and events to facilitate their recovery. The next section discusses why it is important to consider how these emergent capabilities and processes can be sustained.

FROM DISASTER TO DEVELOPMENT

The work discussed above identified how the factors that influenced adaptive outcomes derived from or developed into features and processes (e.g., collective efficacy, sense of community, active participation etc.) characteristic of mainstream community life. For example, people participate with those with whom they identify with in everyday life. In doing so, they collaborate with one another to confront shared issues (i.e., they develop collective efficacy), and they develop a sense of belongingness (sense of community) from their regular interactions with others.

If the processes and characteristics that make a difference derive from or are comparable to everyday community competencies, it follows that a disaster could be used as a catalyst for developing community competencies and social capital. The relation between the everyday and the extraordinary introduces the fact that there is considerable merit in exploring how disaster experience can be used to represent a context for developing future social capital and adaptive capacity. Doing so is especially pertinent in areas such as those discussed above where the risk of experiencing future hazard events is high. That is, the preceding discussion opens opportunities for exploring the benefits that can accrue if risk management policy, planning and intervention strategies accommodate the need to develop sustainable community adaptive capacity as being supplementary to the efforts expended on recovery and reconstruction. It is a logical next step to include discussion of how recovery and future development can be linked.

Disaster and Development

The research discussed in this chapter illustrates how DRR policy, planning and intervention can profit from making more use of community engagement and empowerment principles and strategies designed to develop social and cultural capacities (e.g., International Recovery Forum, 2013; Kapucu and Liu, 2014; Mosel and Levine, 2014; Paton et al. 2014). This goal is increasingly making its presence felt in the DRR space through concepts such as “Build Back Better” (BBB) and “Linking Relief, Rehabilitation and Development” (LRRD). In the final section of this chapter, the LRRD construct is used to frame a discussion of how it may be possible to capitalize on recovery intervention and knowledge to facilitate the development of person- and community-level capabilities in ways that contribute to enhancing sustained DRR in communities that face the prospect of future exposure to disasters.

Linking Relief, Rehabilitation and Development (LRRD)

The LRRD (Linking Relief, Rehabilitation and Development) concept (Buchanan-Smith and Fabbri, 2005; Christoplos, 2006; Mosel and Levine, 2014) emerged from recognition of problems reconciling the ever-growing incidence and intensity of disasters and social and physical consequences they leave in their wake with the corresponding increased need for and spiralling costs of post-event relief and reconstruction (Buchanan-Smith and Maxwell, 1994; Kapucu and Liou, 2014). Recent work on LRRD argues that linking relief and development can mitigate demands on emergency relief, contribute to development and better rehabilitation and facilitate the transition rehabilitation and development. (Kapucu and Liou, 2014; Mosel and Levine, 2014). The LRRD concept can be operationalized and used (Mosel and Levine, 2014) to provide a framework for exploring how the research findings discussed earlier in this chapter can provide insights into how it can be put into practice.

Mosel and Levine (2014) discuss how a key aspect of LRRD involves integrating the expertise and actions of diverse stakeholders. This is echoed in the multi-level nature of recovery and how empowerment serves to increase the ability of community and societal activities to complement one another to facilitate action. If communities and agencies collaborate to confront issues over time, this can build trust and develop mechanisms to link them. Acknowledgment of the multi-level characteristics of recovery (Kapucu and Liou, 2014) provides a potential framework for dialogue across stakeholder groups (e.g., community, NGOs) at different levels of analysis (see Figure 2).

One advantage of integrating resilience into LRRD is that it stimulates thinking about flexible and adaptable approaches to engaging with routine unpredictability and crises, and people's changing and diverse needs (Kapucu and Liou, 2014) and affords ways of finding *different ways* of thinking about development in the wake of complex, protracted disasters and ensuring that aid is targeted to those most vulnerable (Mosel and Levine, 2014).

The preceding discussion also provides some answers to Mosel and Levine's (2014) call for evidence that investment in agency resilience-building competencies and strategies will provide a return on investment in terms of not just the management of a given event but also in terms of future development.

Across the studies discussed above, empowerment (and trust) emerged as pivotal influences on how the relationships between people, communities and agencies facilitated adaptation by ensuring that responsibility was shared in ways that allowed for complementary action. This draws attention to a need to focus on the benefits that can accrue from switching from engagement as an activity that is agency centred, to one that focuses on improving the lives and capabilities of those affected by disaster through complementary and future-oriented action. Adopting an empowerment-based approach can contribute to the LRRD goal of planning and intervention activities that are 'rights based' and which focus on agency and government actions that facilitate people's ability to claim their rights rather than just meeting (often assumed) needs of affected populations (Mosel and Levine, 2014). Rights-based approaches support linking relief and development by shifting the focus to underlying problems, such as the denial of rights and freedoms that frequently underpin and sustain systemic vulnerability in at risk populations (Christoplos, 2006).

The benefits of this approach are acknowledged in emerging LRRD thinking in terms of the value of incorporating Disaster Risk Reduction (DRR) processes within LRRD plans and strategies (Mosel and Levine, 2014). These authors highlight the role of DRR in reforming how development assistance works through increasing the capacity of at-risk people, communities and societies to anticipate future hazardous circumstances and to develop competencies that facilitate achieving the related goal of early recovery. The inclusion of a DRR component in LRRD also lays a foundation for longer term rehabilitation and development (Mosel and Levine, 2014). This approach can be further supported using a strength-based approach to link recovery and the development of future community capacity (Paton, Jang and Liu, 2016).

A strength-based approach builds on an understanding of the social, cultural and spiritual characteristics of a community and its members (Paton et al. 2016). It assumes that survivors are capable of managing their recovery, but may need to be facilitated in this process (rather than being directed). This includes mobilizing spiritual and cultural beliefs and practices played in people's adaptive responses. This once again reiterates the role of empowerment and the importance of future planning being built on partnerships between community members and agencies. When implemented, strength-based recovery strategies contribute to sustaining the cultural and spiritual integrity of the community, reduce physical and social recovery costs, increase the effectiveness of recovery, and increase the likelihood of building social capital in affected areas. Doing so increases the likelihood of coping and adaptive behaviors maintaining and building on social and cultural identity, with these benefits being perpetuated in improved community-based DRR.

Rehabilitation, Development and Planning

Consistent with contemporary DRR thinking, LRRD involves, as Mosel and Levine (2014) argue, more than a returning to a prior state. It has at its core the goal of motivating, developing and supporting local initiatives, goals and strategies in pursuit of locally-meaningful, sustainable development. That is, an aim is to focus development in ways that builds adaptive capacity through the concerted and complementary actions of diverse stakeholders (see Figures 1 and 2). Disaster recovery and rehabilitation phases can serve as a catalytic context that afford unique opportunities for stakeholders to engage in transformative development (physical and social).

The research discussed above attest to the need for development to include sharing knowledge in ways that encompass the perspectives, needs and knowledge of experts, developers and communities in participative, consultative and engaging ways. Doing so requires the development of relationships and supporting design and evaluation processes based on community-based needs analysis. Such bottom-up analyses inform the development of the kind of participative decision making capabilities and processes that increase the likelihood of lessons from past events being both learned and encapsulated in the social and cultural fabric of communities (see strength-based approach above). It follows from the latter that, to be effective, such processes must also be able to extract, document and use indigenous knowledge, practices and social structures.

The inclusion of resilience and adaptive capacity as guiding concepts can facilitate the development of core attributes of effective LRRD (Mosel and Levine, 2014). This includes building in flexibility to increase capacity to adapt to unpredictable response and rehabilitation circumstances and to tailor agency-community interactions in ways that more readily complement one another, with social media affording new opportunities to achieve these objectives. To pursue this goal, changes in organizational culture may be required, particularly with regard to organizations adopting a culture that embraces risk taking and openness to learning as core cultural attributes. This point is reinforced in the studies discussed above. All the studies discussed above emphasized the fact that agency roles extended beyond their just being providers of resources.

The quality of the relationship between people and agency was equally, if not more, important. Factors such as governance strategies, the development of crisis procedures and staff training need to be considered if agencies are to realize their potential as empowering resources that can facilitate both recovery and development. The strengths and weaknesses of community-agency relationships are more transparent in the high demand recovery and rehabilitation contexts, and this can be used to explore ways of developing agency capabilities and nurturing sustainable and enduring links with formal and informal local institutions and organizations, NGOs, civil society groups, traditional authorities, tribal and clan structures, and businesses. Crucial for such engagement will be a good understanding of local power relations. This can represent a significant challenge to agencies and their staff and calls for them to be more open and reflective about how they engage with and sustain collaborative relationships with local institutions and organisations through joint analysis, planning and learning at country level and the decentralization and devolution of authority (Curnin, Owen, Paton, Trist, and Parsons, 2015; International Recovery Forum, 2013; Mosel and Levine, 2014). Putting these ideas into practice can be advanced by developing consultative strategies that support integration. Scenario planning is one such strategy that has been adopted to support the pursuit of the kind of development goals advocated for by LRRD (Paton, 2014).

CONCLUSION

In an international context in which disasters will not only continue to occur, they will, in all likelihood, become more frequent, more intense and last longer, facilitating the capacity of people, communities and societies to be able to adapt will become increasingly important disaster risk reduction and social policy goals. While it will not be possible to change the hazards people may experience per se, there is much that can be done to influence how people and communities can adapt and develop from their encounters with the challenging consequences and circumstances experienced during and after disaster. The studies discussed above provide insights into the adaptive capacities people and communities have at their disposal to reduce their risk and hasten their recovery should disaster occur. The challenge ahead is developing ways in which these lessons can be sustainably incorporated into the fabric of community and societal life by means that will increase the capability of people and communities to respond to and develop from the disasters that are and that will continue to be all too frequent facets of the lives of peoples around the world.

References

Bannister S., Gledhill K. (2012). Evolution of the 2010–2012 Canterbury earthquake sequence, New Zealand. *Journal of Geology and Geophysics,* 55:3, 295-304.

Behling, O., and McFillen, J. M. (1996). A syncretical model of charismatic/transformational leadership. *Group and Organization Management,* 21(2), 163-191. doi: 10.1177/1059601196212004.

Belblidia, M. S. (2010). Building community resilience through social networking sites: Using online social networks for emergency management. *International Journal of Information Systems for Crisis Response and Management,* 2(1), 24-36. doi: 10.4018/jiscrm.2010120403.

Beyerlein, K., and Sikkink, D. (2008). Sorrow and solidarity: Why Americans volunteered for 9/11 relief efforts. *Social Problems,* 55(2). doi 190-215. 10.1525/sp.2008.55.2.190.

Blanchard, H., Carvin, A., Whittaker, M. E., Fitzgerald, M., Harman, W., and Humphrey, B. (2010). White Paper: The Case for Integrating Crisis Response With Social Media. American Red Cross, Retrieved July 6, 2014, from http://www.scribd.com/doc/35737608/White-Paper-The-Case-for-Integrating-Crisis-Response-With-Social-Media.

Bruijn, K.M.D. (2004). Resilience indicators for flood risk management systems of lowland rivers. *International Journal of River Basin Management,* 2, 199-210.

Buchanan-Smith, M. and P. Fabbri (2005) Links between Relief, Rehabilitation and Development in the Tsunami Response: A Review of the Debate. London, Tsunami Evaluation Coalition.

Burke, S., Richardson, J., and Whitton, S. (2013). Psychological first aid: An Australian guide to supporting people affected by disaster. Victoria, Australia: Joint publication of the Australian Pscyhological Society and The Australian Red Cross. Retrieved July 4, 2014, from http://www.psid.org.au/

Carpenter, S., Walker, B., Andries, J.M., and Abel, N. (2001). From metaphor to measurement: Resilience of what to what? Ecosystems, 8, 941-044.

Christoplos, I. (2006) Links between Relief, Rehabilitation and Development in the Tsunami Response: A Synthesis of Initial Findings. London.

Curnin, S., Owen, C., Paton, D., Trist, C. and Parsons, D. (2015) Role Clarity, Swift Trust and Multi-Agency Coordination. *Journal of Contingencies and Crisis Management.* 23, *29-35.*

Department of Premier and Cabinet (2013). *2013* Tasmanian bushfires inquiry report. [Department of Premier and Cabinet Report]. Retrieved June 20, 2014, from http://www.dpac.tas.gov.au/_data/assets/pdf_file/0015/208131/1.Tasmanian_Bushfires_Inquiry_Report.pdf.

Eysenbach, G. (2008). Medicine 2.0: Social networking, collaboration, participation, apomediation, and openness. *Journal of Medical Internet Research,* 10(3), e22. doi:10.2196/jmir.1030.

Eng, E., and Parker, E. (1994). Measuring community competence in the Mississippi Delta: The interface between program evaluation and empowerment. *Health Education Quarterly,* 21(2), 199-220.

Farley, J. E. (1998). Down but not out: Earthquake awareness and readiness trends in the St. Louis metropolitan area, 1990-1997. [survey]. International Journal of Mass Emergencies and Disasters. 16(3), 303-319.

Gaillard, J-C. (2007). Resilience of traditional societies in facing natural hazards. Disaster Prevention and Management, 16, 522-544.

International Recovery Forum (2013) Recommendations for Recovery and Reconstruction in Post-2015 Global Framework for DRR. Kobe, Japan, International Recovery Forum.

Irons, M. (2015) "We can help:" An Australian case study of post-disaster online convergence and community resilience. Unpublished PhD Thesis, Hobart: University of Tasmania.

Jang, L. (2008). Natural disasters: Effects of cultural factors on resilience. North Charleston, SC: VDM Verlag Dr. Muller Aktiengesellschaft and Co. KG and Licensors.

Jang, L. and LaMendola. W. (2006). The Hakka spirit as a predictor of resilience. In D. Paton and D. Johnston. Disaster resilience: An integrated approach. Springfield, IL: Charles C. Thomas.

Jang, L. and LaMendola, W. (2007, Fall), Social work in natural disasters: *The case of spirituality and posttraumatic growth, Advances in Social Work Journal,* 8(2), 67-78.

Kapucu, N. and Liou, K. T. (2014). Disaster and development: Examining global issues and cases. New York, NY: Springer.

Klein, R., Nicholls, R., and Thomalla, F. (2003). Resilience to natural hazards: How useful is this concept? Environmental Hazards, 5, 35-45.

Lin, L. (2002). The statistic analysis of natural disasters in Taiwan and Fu-jian. Taipei, Taiwan: Department of Statistics, Ministry of the Interior. (In Chinese).

Lo, J.C. (2010) The Impact of the Chi-Chi Earthquake on Demographic Changes: An Event History Analysis. in S. Kurosu, T. Bengtsson and C. Campbell (Eds) Demographic Responses to Economic and Environmental Crises. Kashiwa, Chiba, Japan. pp. 193 – 203.

Lowe, S., and Fothergill, A. (2003). A need to help: Emergent volunteer behavior after September 11th. In J. L. Monday (Ed.) Beyond September 11th: An account of post-disaster research (pp. 293-314). Boulder, Colorado: University of Colorado, Institute of Behavioral Science, Natural Hazards Research and Applications Information Center.

Mamula-Seadon, L., Selway, K, and Paton, D. (2012). Exploring Resilience: Learning from Christchurch communities. Tephra, 23, 5-7.

McIvor, D., Paton, D. and Johnston, D.M. (2009) Modelling community preparation for natural hazards: Understanding hazard cognitions. *Journal of Pacific Rim Psychology,* 3, 39-46.

Mosel, I. and Levine, S. (2014) Remaking the case for linking relief, rehabilitation and development. London, Overseas Development Institute.

Nathanson, I. (2003). Spirituality and the life cycle. In T. Tirrito and T. Cascio (Eds.), Religious organizations in community services: A social work perspective (pp. 63-77). New York: Springer

Norris, F.H., Stevens, S.P., Pfefferbaum, B., Wyche, K.F., and Pfefferbaum, R.L. (2008). Community resilience as a metaphor, theory, set of capacities, and strategies for disaster readiness. *American Journal of Community Psychology,* 41, 127-150.

Paton, D. (2006a). Disaster Resilience: Integrating individual, community, institutional and environmental perspectives. In D.Paton and D. Johnston (Eds), Disaster Resilience: An integrated approach. Springfield, Ill.: Charles C. Thomas.

Paton, D. (2006b). Disaster Resilience: Building capacity to co-exist with natural hazards and their consequences. In D.Paton and D. Johnston (Eds), Disaster Resilience: An integrated approach. Springfield, Ill.: Charles C. Thomas.

Paton, D. (2008). Risk communication and natural hazard mitigation: how trust influences its effectiveness. International Journal of Global Environmental Issues, 8, 2-16.

Paton, D. (2014) Disaster Management for Community Workers. Taipei, Taiwan: Ministry of Health and Welfare.

Paton, D. (2012). MCDEM Christchurch Community Resilience Project Report. Wellington, New Zealand: Ministry of Civil Defence and Emergency Management.

Paton, D. and Gow, K. (2008) Rising from the Ashes: Empowering the Phoenix. In K. Gow and D. Paton (Eds) The Phoenix of Natural Disasters: Community resilience. (pp. 1-10) New York: Nova Science Publishers.

Paton, D. and Jang, L. (2011). Disaster Resilience: Exploring All-hazards and Cross Cultural Perspectives. In D. Miller and J. Rivera (Eds), Community Disaster Recovery and Resiliency: Exploring Global Opportunities and Challenges. London: Taylor and Francis.

Paton, D., Jang, L-j, and Liu, L-W (2016) Long-term community recovery: lessons from earthquake and typhoon experiences in Taiwan. In H. James and D. Paton (Eds) The Consequences of Disasters: Demographic, Planning and Policy implications. Springfiled, Ill.: Charles C. Thomas.

Paton, D., Johnston, D., Mamula-Seadon, L and Kenney, C.M. (2014) Recovery and Development: Perspectives from New Zealand and Australia. In Kapucu, N. and Liou, K. T. (Eds). Disaster and development: Examining global issues and cases. New York, NY: Springer (pp. 255-272).

Pelling, M. and High, C. (2005). Understanding adaptation: What can social capital offer assessment of adaptive capacity? Global Environmental Change, 15, 308-319.

Stallings, R. A., and Quarantelli, E. L. (1985). Emergent citizen groups and emergency management. Public Administration Review, 45, Special Issue: Emergency Management: A Challenge for Public Administration, 93-100. https://www.cs.colorado.edu/~palen/starbirdpaleniscramretweet.pdf.

Vieweg, S., Palen, L., Liu, S. B., Hughes, A. L., and Sutton, J. (2008). Collective intelligence in disaster: An examination of the phenomenon in the aftermath of the 2007 Virginia Tech shootings. Proceedings of the 5th International ISCRAM Conference. Retrieved November 1, 2014, from http://amandaleehughes.com/CollectiveIntelligenceISCRAM08.pdf.

World Health Organization (WHO) (2013), Building back better: sustainable mental health care after emergencies. WHO: Geneva.

Yang, W. S. (2004). A census of the Hakka population in Taiwan. Taipei, Taiwan: Council for Hakka Affairs, Executive Yuan, R. O. C. [in Chinese]

In: Capacity Building
Editor: Diane Brown

ISBN: 978-1-63483-995-2

Chapter 6

EFFECTIVE TRAINING TOOLS IN LOCAL AND REGIONAL DEVELOPMENT PLANNING AND MANAGEMENT IN AFRICA*

Asfaw Kumssa
Former Coordinator of United Nations Centre
for Regional Development (UNCRD), Africa Office in Nairobi, Kenya

ABSTRACT

Regional development planning is a conscious development strategy designed to bring about change and equity, and to improve the living standards of people by integrating economic, social and environmental policies and programmes in a spatial context. The focus in this chapter is on theoretical issues of training on Local and regional development planning and management, including the trainers, trainees, the subject matter and the training methods. Case example is drawn from a training course by the United Nations Centre Regional Development, Arica Office on Local and Regional Development Planning and Management. The aim is to explore the scope of training and regional approaches, including the choice of relevant modules/subjects, training methods, training materials and challenges of training the critical mass of planners. Particular attention is given to the importance of regionalization of training in Africa.

* The views expressed here are the author's own and not necessarily those of the United Nations.

Keywords: Regional development planning; development policy; capacity building; United Nations Centre for Regional Development; Africa

I. INTRODUCTION

Training in regional development planning and management is a relatively new field. This is mainly due to the fact that the subject of regional development itself is a relatively new science compared to the other traditional sciences such as economics, geography, public administration, political science and others. Consequently the "roles and functions of regional planners are still obscure" (Rodwin, 1981) and oftentimes overlaps with the roles and activities of other planners from other disciplines.

Therefore designing an effective training course in regional development and management requires clearly demarcating and articulating the subjects that have to be covered and the areas that are relevant to regional development planners. Unless we come to grips with the specific nature of regional development planning and develop a clearer vision of what is expected of regional development planners, the training programme envisioned to improve the skills and knowledge of the participants, will not produce any significant results.

Therefore the first task is to briefly define what regional development planning is and clearly demarcate the difference between regional development and other disciplines that are also dealing with development issues.

According to Friedmann (1966), regional development planning is a planning process that deals with the where of development. It is concerned with socioeconomic and environmental changes in a spatial system or geographical area. In its traditional forms, regional development planning aimed at stimulating development in a backward region through the so called growth pole or growth center strategy (Mabogunje, 1981).

Regional development planning is a conscious strategy designed to bring about change and equity, and to improve the living standards of people by integrating economic, social and environmental policies and programmes in a spatial context. According to Boisier (1981) regional development strategy is the set of measures designed to rationalize the decision making process which originates and controls economic and social change in a spatial system. It deals with the process of economic development in a geographic area, which is a subdivision of a larger national economy. Unlike the national-sectoral development approach, regional development strategy "aims not only at increased welfare in aggregate terms but also at more equitable distribution of it among areas and groups of people" (Misra, 1981: 27). As such, it may address the problems of urbanization, depressed areas, rural-urban migration, unemployment, national economic growth and the like.

By focusing on a specified region or geographical area, regional development promotes community-based and need-oriented development policy. It also focuses on the potential and opportunities that exist at the local level in terms of human resources, infrastructure, institutional capacity, and financial resources and sets the agenda for sustainable development in a given geographic area.

In general it focuses on the processes of planned institutional change to bring about a better correspondence between human needs, including economic security and civil liberties on the one hand, and social policies and programmes on the other in a spatial context. The central feature of a regional-based approach is the emphasis on a people-centred development by empowering local communities, promoting effective participation, fostering the self-organising capability of local people and strengthening local institutions.

In this regard, it provides effective tools and instruments to effectively address poverty, urban and rural linkages, a balanced distribution of population and economic activities in a spatial context to attain equity, and social cohesion. It also promotes participatory planning, an efficient organization of space, more effective incorporation of environmental and disaster risk management factors in an integrated manner and appropriate institutional arrangements to enhance resilience and sustainable development.

Despite these advantages, there is evidence from many African countries that there is need for building capacities at the regional and local levels to face the challenges of regional planning and management, and to attain sustainable development. Effective implementation of regional development policies require responsive institutions and skilled manpower, which oftentimes are lacking in many African countries. There is demand for institutional and technical capacity building to enable these countries to design and implement effective regional development policies and programs, collect and analyze the necessary data for regional plan preparation and to set appropriate instruments at regional and local levels to effectively integrate the three dimensions of sustainable development (economic, social and environment) and to achieve equity, efficiency and sustainability. If development is to be sustained, development planning should incorporate approaches, which strengthen the self-organising capability of local communities and enhance the competency of planners at the regional and local levels. After all, these planners are the ones who are mainly engaged in planning and implementing development projects at the grassroots level. Therefore, regional planners must become intimately familiar with the socioeconomic and cultural settings of the society in which they work in order to bring about change. They must understand the dynamics of their community. This knowledge can be acquired through competency-based training, which in turn can lead to the skilful use of intervention techniques.

The means to bring about this are twofold: international training programmes; and tailor-made courses for specific countries on particular topics. The competency of planners can be further improved by producing effective training materials and textbooks to aid them in their day-to-day activities. Given their crucial role in both planning and implementing development programs, they should have the competence to accomplish these tasks efficiently and effectively. The way to acquire the requisite knowledge and skills is through training.

The expansion of the regional development concept and the recent decentralization trends in Africa, which led to greater devolution power to local and regional entities, have all popularized regional development and increased the rationale for establishing regional development strategies. At the same time, it has also increased the demand for regional planners and consequently the importance of training in regional development and management.

In this chapter, I will first briefly examine some of the theoretical issues involved in training and then discuss case study of the Africa Training Course on Local and Regional Development Planning and Management within the context of this theoretical framework. Finally, I will give some suggestions to improve future training programs and end the chapter with summary and conclusion.

II. Some Conceptual Issues in Training

Training involves the transfer of new knowledge, skills and attitudes to improve trainees' competencies to perform certain specific tasks effectively and efficiently. Unlike education, which is concerned more with the general improvement of knowledge, training focuses on enhancing the skills of individuals for a clearly specified tasks (Hakimian and Teshome, 1993).

As such, training is a learning process. According to Nadler (1982), there are two ways of learning: (1) incidental; and (2) intentional learning.

Incidental learning is the knowledge we acquire through our day-to-day activities such as reading newspapers and magazines, watching television and listening to radio and the like, while intentional learning is a systematic way of acquiring knowledge where an "individual expects to be a learner, where there are identified objectives, where time is devoted to the learning, and some kind of evaluation is planned" (Nadler, 1982: 2).

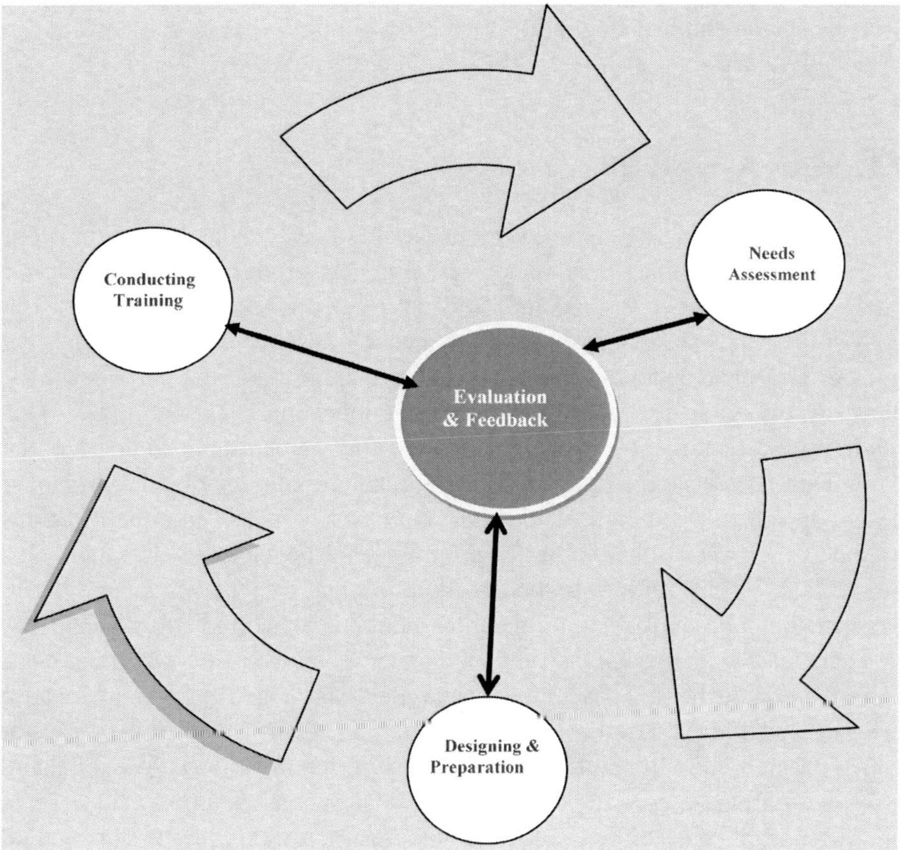

Source: Developed from Hakimian and Teshome (1993) Training Cycles.

Figure 1. The Training Cycle.

Training is an intentional learning process through which trainees acquire the necessary skills, knowledge, and attitude required to accomplish their tasks competently (Jones and Yogo, 1996). Moreover, training is action or specific goal oriented; and the trainees are expected to use the knowledge and skills they have acquired during the training course into practice upon completion of the training program.

According to Hakimian and Teshome (1993), a well designed and systematically structured training programme has four cycles:

(1) Needs assessment;
(2) Designing and preparation;
(3) Conducting training; and
(4) Evaluation.

2.1. Needs Assessment

Prior to conducting a training program, it is crucial to make needs assessment. According to Nadler, the term needs refer to "the difference between a goal (what is expected) and what actually exists" (1982:84). The goal of the needs assessment involves collecting baseline data, identifying the trainees and their needs in order to get information about the gaps that exist between the goal set and the state of affairs that actually exist. This pre-training assessment activities will give the trainers an insight into the participants' needs and educational background and thus enable the formers to design an effective training course that will meet the needs and qualifications of the participants of the training programme. The baseline data will also provide the state of affairs before intervention and thus makes it possible to evaluate the progress made after the intervention is made (the training course).

One of the important aspects of the needs assessment phase includes identification of the trainees and their qualifications. This is important because prior to launching a training programme one has to first identify the levels at which the training will be offered and clearly define the knowledge, skills and attitude the trainees need to accomplish their tasks competently. Since trainees are different in terms of their educational background, experience, age, and all the like when designing a training program, the trainer has to have a detailed background information about the participants.

The other important aspect of needs assessment is the identification of the tasks that the trainees have to perform upon completion of their training programs. In case of social development, Jones and Yogo (1994) divide the tasks of the development worker into two major categories:

(1) Generic tasks; and
(2) Operational tasks:
   (a) Complex tasks
   (b) Routine tasks

Generic tasks involve planning and management aspect of development activities; and therefore, the emphasis here is on theoretical and management skills of development workers. On the other hand, operational tasks refer to the activities of development workers which involve direct interaction with the community. The operational tasks are further divided into two categories: complex and routine tasks. Complex tasks are activities, which involve difficult and complex assignments while routine tasks are simple and routine activities (Jones and Yogo, 1996).

2.2. Designing and Preparation

The next step in conducting training is to prepare the training program that includes defining the objectives, designing the curriculum and preparing training materials. All these activities are designed based on and in accordance with the information gathered during the needs assessment phase. One of the important aspects of this phase is designing the curriculum. A curriculum is the outline of the content of the course to be taught during the training program. Its content is determined by the objective of the training program, and depends upon the tasks that are to be performed by the trainees. A well designed and systematically prepared curriculum should clearly state the course outline and the methodology of teaching. It should also clearly demarcate the relative importance of each section of the curriculum and establish a systematic sequence in which each section should be delivered.

When designing a training curriculum, Jones and Yogo (1994) suggest that the curriculum be prepared based on the tasks to be performed by the trainees at the end of the training program. In this regard, the skills, knowledge and attitudes that the trainees need to acquire to perform their job tasks competently should be reflected in the content of the curriculum.

One of the factors that determine the quality and effectiveness of a training program is the methodology it uses. At the preparatory stage, the methodology of the training course should be clearly articulated and made known to the participants as well the resource persons. Different training programs have their own methods of conducting training but generally it is preferred to have an interactive and output-oriented methodology.

2.3. Conducting Training

Once the training program is systematically organized, it is ready to be delivered. It could be conducted in the form of lectures, workshops, seminars and all the like. Hakimian and Teshome (1993), identify the following nine presentation techniques:

(1) Lecture
(2) Demonstration
(3) Discussion
(4) Case Study
(5) Role Play
(6) Simulation
(7) Games
(8) Brainstorming
(9) Buzz Group

Also, it is important to note that today with the technological innovation made in the area of telecommunication, the method of conducting training cannot be limited to in-class or face-to-face training. It could be effectively conducted through distance training utilizing television, video, Internet, radio (Jones and Kumssa, 1996). In fact, in many countries distance training is becoming the most convenient and cost effective method of conducting training courses.

2.4. Evaluation and Feedback

The final phase of a training program is evaluation to assess the effectiveness of the training program. This is important because training does not automatically improve the skills and knowledge of all trainees and therefore evaluation should be carried out to assess the impact of course on individual participants. A standardized and reliable method must be designed to evaluate the outcome and success of the training program. What is being evaluated is the outcome of the training programme and the performance of the trainees in relation to mastery of the training program and its content (Jones and Yogo, 1994). Nadler (1982) identifies four major objectives of evaluation to:

(1) Determine if the training program meets the needs and criteria established by earlier events;
(2) Identify those individuals who should have been involved, and receive specific feedback from them;
(3) Modify the training program, as appropriate, based on the feedback from selected individuals; and
(4) Obtain necessary approval from those concerned to proceed with the next event of the training design.

During the evaluation phase, the data and information gathered after the intervention is compared with the baseline data to evaluate the success and failure of the training program.

III. Africa Training Course on Local and Regional Development Planning and Management

The United Nations Centre for Regional Development (UNCRD) in Nagoya, Japan, was established in 1971 by an agreement between the UN and the Japanese government. Its purpose is to assist and promote regional development in developing countries, a concept and practice that has further evolved over the years UNCRD has four responsibilities: training and research; advisory services; information dissemination; and cooperation with other UN and international organizations, national and local governments, and civil society organizations concerned with regional development to promote regional development in developing countries.

The United Nations Centre for Regional Development (UNCRD) Africa was established in 1992 in Nairobi Kenya to serve as UNCRD's regional office for Africa. Since its establishment in 1992, UNCRD Africa Office had been supporting African countries in their endeavor to design and implement effective regional development plans and policies by undertaking training, research and technical assistance in local and regional development. The main objective of the Office is to support African countries to achieve economic recovery and long-term sustainable development through training, policy research, and technical advisory services on effective management strategies for regional and national development. The Office aims to complement the efforts of other international development organizations, government and non-governmental organizations (NGOs), and other local institutions.

Responding to multifaceted regional and domestic crises and a liberalizing global order, a growing number of African countries began restructuring their institutional frameworks to facilitate more sustainable economic, social and political development. Several important trends can be discerned in this process: a movement towards decentralization; devolution of bureaucratic powers; progress towards better governance and grassroots participation; and initiatives to strengthen sub-national planning to stimulate sustainable local and regional development. Reforms include the devolution and delegation of government functions to local and regional authorities to encourage community-based participatory development; administrative decentralization to improve accountability; efficiency and effectiveness; the creation or revitalization of local development initiatives to meet the real needs of the people; promotion of the private sector to improve efficient resource allocation and utilization; and increasing sensitivity to gender issues and the interests of vulnerable groups.

Most importantly, with the collapse of the central planning system and the advent of a new global order, many African countries accepted economic liberalization and democratization of their polity as a prerequisite to sustainable development. Therefore, they began to pay more attention to good governance and devolution of power to local and regional authorities. Along this line there are important political changes with democratic governments emerging in many parts of Africa. Many of the African countries, which in the past embarked upon state controlled development, have embraced liberalization and devolved decision-making authority to regional and local governments. These political and economic changes have brought both opportunities and challenges for African countries.

The opportunities include but not limited to democratization and strengthening local governance because, as a participatory process, decentralization empowers local-level authorities and communities to participate in the decision-making process that affect their community, including designing and implementing of development programs as well as participating in the political process. The act of allowing local and regional authorities and governments to share power with the central government, enables local governance not only to nurture democracy by enhancing grassroots participation in the political process of a country, but also to create an environment where development plans become more responsive to local conditions and needs by strengthening the role civil society organizations play in the economic, social and political life of the people at the local level.

On the other hand, one of the challenges facing African countries moving to decentralized government administration and development is the severe lack of trained manpower with expertise in local and regional development planning and management at the local and regional levels. With decentralization and devolution of power to local and regional authorities, the demand for regional planners is on the rise. However, these increased demands for qualified regional planners are largely unmet. The unmet demands reduce the effective design and implementation of regional development programs.

The training program of UNCRD Africa Office was designed to equip mid-career planners with an analytical framework and tools to design and implement effective regional development policies and programs. The cardinal objective of the Africa Training Course on Local and Regional Development Planning and Management is to strengthen the institutional capacity of African countries in local and regional development planning and management and supports their on-going policy reforms designed to accelerate economic growth, reduce existing socioeconomic and regional inequality, alleviate poverty and promote sustainable development.

In 1995, the United Nations Centre for Regional Development (UNCRD) Africa Office organized the first Africa Training Course (ATC) on Local and Regional Development Planning in Nairobi, Kenya. Nineteen (19) participants from thirteen (13) African countries attended the course. The Second Africa Training Course, held in Harare, Zimbabwe in 1996, was attended by twenty-two (22) participants from fourteen (14) African countries. Since then the Africa Training Course had been organized in Nairobi, Kenya until 2014 when the UNCRD Africa Office was closed down due to financial difficulties.

It is recognized that in several African countries some form of training is organized for development planners. However, most of the training programs that exist accommodate only the interests of higher education rather than the regional development field where local or regional level personnel are engaged. Those who work directly with the local communities, the poor and implement development projects at the local or regional levels find themselves ignored by the majority of universities and colleges. In this regard, there is clearly a training gap to be filled.

Preliminary estimates of the numbers of regions, provinces, districts, divisions, and municipalities in Africa suggest that the continent could absorb several thousand new local and regional planners each year (Gates, 2001). Universities and training institution, even those offering regional development planning, are not prepared, either in program structure or capacity, to produce the graduates to meet this unmeet demand.

Africa Training Course on Local and Regional Development Planning and Management was designed to fill this gap. It was organized and implemented by UNCRD Africa Office, in collaboration with its partners. The ATC consists of multiple activities that are inter-linked and mutually reinforcing. The core program is the ATC while the other interlinked activities include: (1) in-country training programs; (2) growing institutional linkage and collaboration with key training and planning centers in Africa and Asia; (2) Exchange of Asia-Africa development experiences; (3) Preparation of improved training material and case studies, including training manuals; and (4) building a broad network of development planners and managers in Africa.

ATC is a tailor-made programme that has been adopted to meet the regional planning needs of African countries in terms of its overall program content, design of its methodology, case study and course material development, Africa-Asia exchange programme; and the added dimension to foster cross-country institutional linkages.

The principal objective of the Africa Training Course is to provide mid-career planners with requisite knowledge and analytical skills in formulating and implementing effective local and regional development policies and plans. Specifically the course has the following objectives:

- Strengthening the institutional capacity of African countries by training planners from government and other relevant institutions/organisations in the essential skills and approaches necessary for effective local and regional development planning and management;
- Enhancing the capacity of training and research institutions in Africa by involving them in preparation and delivery of training modules for planners;
- Creating a forum in the context of the ATC in which African planners can exchange views and comparative experiences, thereby promoting network-building among relevant institutions and personnel in Africa;
- Providing African planners with exposure, through *inter alia*, study tours, to the lessons and experiences of Asia's development strategies and other regions from which they can draw useful lessons; and

- To provide training of trainers (TOT) with alumni serving as resource persons to organise and deliver local in-country training programmes reaching a much larger constituency.

3.1. Participants

Participants are mainly mid-career planners from but not limited to national and local government agencies, research and training institutes, universities and NGOs. Nomination of the participants is made through governments of African countries, multilateral and bilateral organizations. The criteria for selection of participants includes strong educational background (a bachelor's degree or equivalent); adequate work experience, physical and mental fitness; and UNCRD's age limit requirement which is between 30-45 years of age. The participants should also prepare and submit country reports as instructed by UNCRD Africa Office.

The participants are those who are involved in actual planning and are able to share their experiences with their fellow colleagues upon returning to their respective workstations. The training course aims at strengthening the institutional capacity of participating countries to design and implement effective regional development policies and programs. To mainstream gender and achieve gender balance, countries and institutions have been encouraged to nominate more women for the course. In selecting participants, the principle applied is to target and focus on the most relevant institutions of the participating country where impact could be made. By targeting designated and lead institution(s) responsible for local and regional development planning on an annual basis, the accumulation of a critical mass of trainers would be achieved. Increasingly, participants were also selected with the Training of Trainers (TOT) principle in mind and with a view to strengthening linkages among key national institutions with responsibilities for training and research, planning, co-ordination and management of local and regional development. This has the potential to provide the continuity and sustainability for in-country training programmes.

3.2. Training Modules

The course was organized around nine distinct but interrelated modules. The course modules were designed to expose participants to the basic tenets of regional development concepts and theories; regional development policies and strategies, the rationale for pursuing regional development policy, regional planning tools and techniques, data collection and analysis, sectoral issues, development administration and social development, project planning and management; and computer gaming and simulation. The modules also ensure that emerging issues in local and regional development are adequately covered. The sequence of modules relates to the practical process of regional development planning which links knowledge to action and theory to practice.

Module 1: Concepts and Issues of Development

The purpose of this module is to expose and sensitize participants to current and emerging issues of development. The module covers current and emerging concepts and theories of development, experiences of different countries, rationale for and underlying themes of regional development planning and management.

Module 2: Fundamentals of Regional Development

This module covers the dimensions of local and regional development: economic, spatial, social, and environmental and how they relate in building a regional development framework. It also covers techniques for regional analysis, participatory techniques, geographical information systems (GIS) and remote sensing in local and regional development planning and management.

Module 3: Sectoral Issues and Planning

The focus in this module is the identification of alternative and complementary strategies to enhance local and regional development. The module includes analysis of critical sectors and policy issues in regional development; planning for strategic sectors including industrial, agriculture, infrastructure, social and environmental management; and major development strategies of regional development.

Module 4: Field Study

The purpose of this module is to expose and give participants practical experience in analyzing real life situations. Participants will be afforded the opportunity to make a field study to selected projects to collect information, evaluate the projects, and prepare group reports and proposals for improvement.

Module 5: Development Administration and Analysis of Micro-base for Local and Regional Development

The focus in this module is to understand and explore the institutional and social capacities available for local and regional development planning and management in African countries. These capacities can be divided into two: the delivery system (development administration) and the receiving system (the micro-base) for local and regional development planning and management. Emphasis will be given on sharing of experiences and lessons in the design and implementation of the decentralization programmes in Africa.

Module 6: Exchange of Asia – Africa Experiences

The purpose of this module is to facilitate exchange of ideas and experiences between Asia and Africa on local and regional development planning and management through lectures, workshops, panel discussions, and analysis of cases. An overview of approaches to regional development planning and management is given with an emphasis on recent experiences in Africa and Asia.

Module 7: Project Planning, Management and Evaluation

In this module, participants are trained on how to link government policy and peoples' needs through project identification, preparation and implementation management, including feasibility studies, cost-benefit analysis, project monitoring and evaluation.

Module 8: Gaming and Simulation

Participants conduct a microcomputer based gaming and simulation exercise on planning process. It is intended to demonstrate the complexities of the decision-making and planning processes at the regional level. Through the gaming and simulation exercise, participants are given an opportunity to enhance their negotiation skills through role-playing and group interaction.

Module 9: Re-entry Planning

Participants are trained on how to organize and conduct in-country training on relevant topics in their respective countries. In this regard, they are introduced to TOT techniques and trained on how to design and deliver in-country training programs. Towards this goal participants prepare and present action plans on how they will utilize lessons learnt during the course when they return to their workstations. This consists of identification of relevant topics and skills, and tasks to be achieved when they re-enter their work. A checklist of these tasks and skills will be a product that each participant can take home and share with his/her colleagues.

3.3. Training Methodology

The course utilized a combination of training techniques including lectures, workshops, group and panel discussions, computer gaming and simulation, case study analysis, and field study. The training methods are participatory and output-oriented, based on three-way dialogue. At the end of each day's topic, working groups meet to synthesize the lessons learnt. Results and feed-back are presented at week-end plenary sessions, using module synthesis worksheets, at which lecturers and resource persons are present in order to ensure that full understanding has been achieved. This three-way dialogue is designed to link key points from the lectures with the issues, tasks, and skills identified by participants, followed by feedback and supplementary input by lecturers and resource persons. This approach ensures *internalization* of the training, and is more effective than conventional techniques.

The training method also includes the case method and case analysis, which will enable participants to make generalization from a particular incident of development in a specific country or community. The conventional training method, which is based on theory and the common literature of regional development, is a poor substitute for a case method (Jones and Yogo, 1994). The case method has clear advantages over more abstract ways of learning when the aim is to acquire competence for specific objective. In this regard, the case method is very effective in knowledge acquisition and retention, attitude change, problem-solving ability and interpersonal skills, which are crucial for regional planners involved in designing and implementing complex projects at the local and regional levels. However, this should not by any means imply undermining the role of theory and conceptual issues since theoretical and conceptual issues have also a pivotal role in improving the knowledge and skills of regional planners. What this means is that the two should compliment and support each other to enhance the knowledge and skills of regional planners.

3.4. Strengthening Africa-Asia Co-Operation

The Africa-Asia Exchange program is, *inter alia* a complementary approach within the context of the South-South cooperation, towards enhanced development cooperation between Asian and African countries, through exchange of experiences in development planning at both local and regional levels.

These exchange programs are designed to promote technical cooperation between Asian and African countries and promote south-south cooperation. The outcome is to be seen within a globalization context that is shifting the global world order towards regional cooperation and integration as part of the larger globalization process.

The globalization process is envisaged to have the dual impact of marginalization of some of the developing countries, especially those with limited productive capacities and trading capabilities, while at the same time creating for others wider markets for trade, larger capital inflows and improved access to new technologies. Within this context, development cooperation among the developing countries, particularly between Asia and Africa, becomes one of the critical and viable options towards accelerated economic growth and sustainable development.

It is in this context that the UNCRD Africa Office initiated and supported the Exchange of Asian and African experiences as part of the south-south cooperation. This was materialized through a series of exchange study tours involving senior scholars and policymakers from Asian and African countries and preparation of series of country case studies. The scholars and policymakers involved also serve as resource persons in the UNCRD's annual training course on Local and Regional Development Planning and Management.

The Africa-Asia Exchange entails exchange of information and experiences on local and regional development planning and management in the two regions, through institutional linkages involving research, training and planning institutes. The participating senior policymakers and scholars are expected to facilitate the transfer of knowledge and lessons learnt from the planning, implementation and management of the development processes and activities in the two regions. This two-way flow of planners, scholars and policymakers will also strengthen institutional linkages between Africa and Asia, and thereby increase Africa's capacity to learn from the experiences of Asian countries.

3.5. Training Faculty and Inter-Institutional Co-Operation

The training staff consisted of UNCRD experts and resource persons invited from key research and training institutions of Africa (Botswana, Ethiopia, Democratic Republic of Congo, Ghana, Kenya, Ghana, South Africa, Uganda and Zimbabwe) and Asia (Australia, India, Japan, Malaysia, the Philippines, Singapore; and Thailand). Participation of the institutions was designed to further contribute to institutional capacity building through their subsequent involvement in the in-country training and Africa-Asia Exchange programmes. The resource persons included both scholars from research and training institutions as well as policymakers from various government institutions. Regional and local development are practiced in different environment of each country, based on respective historical, social and cultural settings. Therefore, there are no clear-cut solutions which all countries may follow. Instead, each country needs to pursue its own way of maximizing effectiveness in local and regional development initiatives. This is another challenge faced by developing countries in promoting decentralization and local governance. South-South cooperation can work in an effective way in bringing countries from different regions to learn from each other, share good practices and failures. This learning process will be reflected in policy formulation and program implementation. Africa-Asia partnership in regional and local development will add a new picture to South-South cooperation due to the contrast of the two regions in terms of historical background as well as common challenges in the needs for capacity development in local and regional development.

3.6. Preparation of Training Materials

Because of the paucity of training materials, there was need to systematically publish relevant and effective training material and case studies to improve both ATC and the in-country training. In this regard, UNCRD Africa Office has collaborated with African and Asian scholars and planners to develop adequate training material for the training programs.

The following textbooks and training materials were developed and published and were used in various training programmes:

(a) Basic training material for all the nine modules of the ATC had been developed by resource persons and these were continuously updated every year.
(b) Ewaso Ng'iro North Development Authority Integrated Regional Development Plan: 2010–2040, Nairobi, UNCRD, 2014.
(c) Kwale District and Mombasa Mainland South Regional Physical Development Plan, 2004 – 2034," Nairobi, UNCRD, 2012.
(d) Regional Development Policies and Practices in Africa and Asia: A Comparative Study, UNCRD Textbook Series No.6. September 2000.
(e) Project Planning, Implementation and Evaluation: A Training Manual, UNCRD Textbook series, No. 8 September 2000.
(f) Regional Development Plan for Hardap Region, Namibia, UNCRD Textbook Series No. 7, April 2000.

(g) Regional Development Policy in Africa: Problems and Prospects Towards the 21st Century, UNCRD Proceedings Series No. 29, 1998;
(h) Regional Development Profile of Ewaso Ng'iro North River Basin in Kenya, UNCRD Research Series No. 28, 1999.
(i) Decentralization and Citizen Participation in Africa, A Special Volume of Regional Development Dialogue, Vol. 21, No. 1, Spring 2000, UNCRD.

3.7. In-Country Training Programmes

ATC is supplemented by in-country training programs, which are conducted in selected African countries. In-country training programs are tailor-made training courses for a specific country on specific subject or topic. Successful in-country training programs were initiated and implemented in Botswana, Ethiopia, Kenya and Namibia.

The rationale for conducting in-country training programs, includes among others:

- Many regional planners can be trained at the same time, and thus in terms of training the critical mass, it has maximum impact; and
- In-country training is specific and tailor-made and therefore it meets the specific needs of each country or region.

When conducting in-country training, UNCRD Africa Office targeted African countries, which embarked upon decentralization programs and are implementing regional development programs. Through its in-country training programmes, UNCRD Africa Office trained a number of regional planners in the four African countries (Botswana, Ethiopia, Kenya and Namibia).

Botswana: The in-country training program in Botswana was designed and implemented to assist the Government of Botswana in its endeavor to train the critical mass of regional planners at the district levels since the country faced a shortage of trained manpower particularly in the area of district and regional planning, including project planning and management and data collection and analysis. All planners, who work for the government at ministerial and district levels, have only a first degree or equivalent level of education in planning. Beyond this, only a few have had opportunities to acquire new planning skills by attending specialized training courses where their planning capacity is improved. Cognizant of this problem and the need to improve district development planning, implementation and monitoring, the Ministry of Local Government, the Government of Botswana requested UNCRD Africa Office to provide technical support and train its planners to enhance their competency in district and regional planning. Towards this objective, UNCRD Africa Office initiated an in-country training programme in Botswana and conducted the first training course in November 2008. The training course targeted district planning officers responsible for district development planning and district projects implementation and management as well as officials responsible for the coordination of development projects. The main objective of the training workshop was to train the planners and government officials in effective district and regional development planning and project planning and management. Through this in-country training, UNCRD Africa Office trained a number of district development planners. The technical assistance, which was implemented in partnership with UNDP Botswana and University of Botswana, continued until 2013 when it was suspended due to financial constraints.

Ethiopia: The in-country training program in Ethiopia aimed at supporting the Regional State of Oromia in its human resource development capabilities and to ensure the availability of skilled manpower and training materials in the region. A major challenge facing the regional governments of Ethiopia is the severe lack of trained manpower in the area of project planning and management and data collection and analysis for plan preparation. In most of these regional states, regional development planners are in short supply, and therefore personnel who lack the necessary skills and expertise in regional development planning, including project planning and management often undertake regional planning activities. In this respect, capacity building was required at all levels of the administrative hierarchy, including at the national, regional and sub-regional levels. Oromia Regional State is the largest region both in terms of population and geographical size. Like any other region in Ethiopia, the regional state is faced with a growing demand for qualified regional planners with requisite skills in project planning and management as well as techniques of data collection and analysis. The technical assistance of UNCRD Africa Office in Ethiopia was designed to fill this gap and provide the planners of the Regional State of Oromia with requisite knowledge and technical know-how to design, implement; and manage effective regional development projects and programs. The training course was also designed to provide the planners and development managers of the regional state of Oromia with appropriate and effective data collection and analysis techniques. Since the in-country training course was launched in 1999 a number of planners had been trained and the institutional capacity of the regional state of Oromia had been strengthened. This was indicated in the two evaluations conducted by the regional government of Oromia to assess the impact of the training course both on individual planners as well as the institutions where they are working. The technical assistance program in Ethiopia lasted from 1999 until 2011.

Kenya: The technical assistance in Kenya focused on building the capacity of Ewaso Ng'iro North Development Authority and Kwale District and Mombasa Mainland South with a preparation of integrated regional development plans. UNCRD's technical assistance program to ENNDA focused on knowledge and skills development as well as institutional building to enable ENNDA to effectively address the problems and challenges of development in the region as a whole. The program was organized around two intertwined components, namely: (i) training; and (ii) regional plan preparation. In the training component, the planners and development managers were trained in emerging concepts and techniques of regional development planning, including data collection and management; environmental issues and natural resource analysis and appraisal; and ecological protection of watershed regions, etc. Similarly, policymakers, including local politicians and community leaders were sensitized on regional framework and approaches to river basin development and sustainable utilization of the natural resources and protecting the environment. In the regional plan preparation component, UNCRD Africa Office provided technical support to the planners and development managers in regional plan preparation, including administrative and legal processes of plan approval. The policymakers were sensitized on a regional approach to development and contributed their inputs into the draft regional plan at appropriate stages and phases of plan preparation process. UNCRD Africa Office, jointly with ENNDA and in collaboration with University of Nairobi, conducted several workshops and seminars to train the planners of ENNDA and sensitize the community towards preparation of an integrated Master Plan for ENNDA. The regional plan titled "*Ewaso Ng'iro North Development Authority Integrated Regional Development Plan: 2010–2040*" was published and launched in 2013.

UNCRD Africa Office also closely worked with the Department of Physical Planning, Ministry of Lands, Housing; and Urban Development and supported the preparation of a regional plan for Kwale District and Mombasa Mainland South. The regional plan titled "*Kwale District and Mombasa*

Mainland South Regional Physical Development Plan, 2004 – 2034" was published and launched in 2012.

Namibia: The state of decentralization in Namibia, although on the right track, left a lot to be desired. Determined, concerted and premeditated efforts were needed to gear the whole process in favor of devolution. The process of decentralization was in operation for many years with a range of functions already decentralized by delegation to Regional and Local Authorities. However, the real function was more of a de-concentrated and sector-approach-type.

Despite the establishment of local planning institutional structures, inter-sectoral co-ordination between sectors and other development partners (including NGOs, CBOs, Traditional Authorities, etc.) was low and somewhat non-existent. The policy framework in place was still to be internalized by many government agencies for it to function fully. Inadequacy of manpower and institutional capacities, especially at regional and local levels continued to be major challenges of effective decentralization. Since 1993, UNCRD Africa Office had been providing technical assistance to the Government of Namibia to enhance the human and institutional capacity of the Ministry of Regional and Local Government, Housing and Rural Development to effectively implement the country's decentralization policy as well as local and regional development programs. The overall aim of the technical assistance program was to strengthen the capacity of the government in the areas of decentralization and regional development programs. Towards these objectives, the technical assistance program focused on human resource development for capacity building by targeting regional officials, regional councilors and governors.

The program also attempted to build the institutional capacity of local and regional authorities by enhancing their capacity to carry out effective policy analysis and identify alternative and complementary strategies for effective local and regional development, project planning, monitoring and evaluation. The Government of Namibia recognized that the capacity building programme had tremendous impact on improving the skills of its officials and producing the critical mass of planners required to undertake decentralization and regional development programs. The planners are utilizing the skills and knowledge they acquired in their day-to-day activities. The training also improved the capacity of the institutions where the planners come from in producing effective plans, projects and programmes. Despite the importance of the in-country training programme in enhancing the skills of the Namibian planners in the field of regional planning and decentralization, the capacity building programme had to be suspended in 2013 due UNCRD's budget constraints.

3.8. Evaluation of the Training Courses

Evaluation is generally undertaken to assess the effectiveness of a training programme and monitor whether the objectives set out are meet. In this regard, evaluation is conducted from two perspectives: the trainees' and the trainers' and their institutions' standpoint. As rightfully indicated by Edralin, "evaluation should focus as much on the trainer as the trainees" (1996:166). The objective of the evaluation, as indicated earlier is to modify and improve a training program. In this regard, ATC was subjected to two types of evaluations: an internal and external/independent evaluation of the training course. Internal evaluation is conducted at the end of each training course. Specially prepared evaluation questionnaires were distributed to the participants of the training course and they were requested to evaluate the training programme in terms of its methodology, course content, lecture material, lecture delivery, organization, etc.

In addition to the internal evaluation, an independent evaluation (external evaluation) team was evaluating the training program twice in three years time. The first mid-term evaluation was undertaken in 1998 and assessed the ATC concept and implementation system, with a special emphasis on issues such as efficiency, effectiveness, impact, relevance and sustainability. The evaluation report indicated the project had positive impact on three distinctly different, but closely related areas: the skills and knowledge of the individual participants who were trained through the course; the institutional capacity of the organizations that employ them; and the capacity of emerging in-country centers of excellence to mount in-country training programmes.

Most of the recommendations pointed out to the need for expanding in-country training activities and building partnerships with in-country centers of excellence (Botswana, Ethiopia, Kenya; and Namibia) and other local stakeholders (local and national government and UN agencies, NGOs, and other international organizations) to help organize and deliver local in-country training with ATC alumni serving as resource persons.

3.9. Building a Network of Development Planners and Managers in Africa

Linkages among development planning personnel in Africa are very weak. Therefore the UNCRD Africa Office endeavored to strengthen linkages among development planning personnel in Africa and to build-up a network of such professionals, which is important for sharing of experiences and information to effectively respond to the development challenges of Africa countries. Towards this goal:

- A database of all past participants of Africa Training Course had been developed and the association of alumni had been formed;
- The network of Africa planners had been enhanced further through the publication of the *ATC Alumni Newsletter*.

3.9.1. ATC Alumni Newsletter

The publication aimed at disseminating the activities of former participants of the Africa Training Course (ATC) as well as the activities of UNCRD Africa Office. The newsletter was published biannually and each issue would feature the activities of UNCRD Africa Office, the profile of former participants, the activities they are undertaking in their current positions and the challenges they are facing in their day-to-day activities.

The aim of the newsletter is to:

- Link former participants of ATC;
- Serve as a tracer of the alumni;
- Provide professional and information network; and
- Promote and initiate programs that will provide continued training and education of the alumni through various UNCRD activities, including in-country training programs.

IV. The Way Forward

While the annual ATC sharpened the skills and the focus of Africa planners, there was urgent need to train the critical mass for bridging the unmet demand in regional planners in Africa. In this regard training of trainers (TOT) approach, coupled with intensive in-country training activities should be emphasized. This would increase the chances of training a critical mass of planners at national and regional levels, and thereby enhance impact of the training programme. The importance of TOT and effectiveness of in-country training are well recognized among regional planners. For instance, Gruchman (1981) believes that country specific trainings are the most successful training courses. He also think that the most important and urgent task of international training centers such as UNCRD should be "training of trainers and training organizers in regional planning" (Gruchman, 1981:190). Along this line, UNCRD Africa Office revised and improved its curriculum by including TOT techniques and means and ways of conducting in-country training. Towards this goal participants prepared and presented actions plans on how they would utilize lessons learnt during the training course when they return to their respective workstations.

UNCRD Africa Office recognized that considerable training, beyond the scope of the annual ATC would be necessary in order to meet the demand for qualified regional planners. Conducting in-country training on a sustainable basis would require capacity building and institutional linkages to support this effort. In this regard, UNCRD Africa Office closely worked with country centers of excellence and ATC alumni and support them in their endeavor to design and implement sustainable in-country training programmes.

Further strengthening institutional linkages with Asian research, training and planning agencies such as National Development Planning Agency (BAPPENAS), Indonesia; the National Economic and Development Authority (NEDA), the Philippines; National Economic and Social Development Board (NESDB), Thailand); and Economic Planning Unit (EPU), Malaysia was necessary to promote cross-fertilization of ideas and experiences of good practices in regional development planning.

All these activities, including the expansion of in-country training and the Asia-Africa exchange programme, entailed additional expenditures and qualified trainers as well as effective and tailor-made instruction materials. To meet these challenges new modes of cooperation and training techniques could have been designed. While strengthening its cooperation with multilateral and bilateral agencies, UNCRD should have gone beyond the traditional field of collaboration and embrace the private sector and NGOs and work closely with them in designing and implementing training as well as research programmes.

UNCRD should have also tried to explore non-traditional but more cost effective and efficient ways of conducting training such as distance training. The revolution made in telecommunication, including the Internet, video, television, have all made distance training very convenient and cost effective in terms training the critical mass and reaching a large number of audience (Jones and Kumssa, 1996). Today, not only training but buying and selling of goods and services through telephone and the Internet have become very common; and tele-conferencing, distance education through video and television, and even tele-working have become cost-effective and widespread practices.

There was also consensus among the ATC course participants and alumni that regional development practitioners should be trained to work in a multidisciplinary team. Trainees needed to hone their skills in analysis, problem solving, negotiation, and communication. The goal of training should be designed to turn out practitioners with generalist rather than specialized skills, since the constant change in the work environment and the multiplicity of tasks make specialized training less relevant in an international course (Jones and Kumssa, 2008).

SUMMARY AND CONCLUSION

The Africa Training Course on Local and Regional Development Planning and Management aimed at improving the planning skills of mid-career planners, administrators, trainers and researchers involved in designing and implementing regional development projects and programmes. The training was designed to enable the participants acquire the skills, knowledge, and attitudes required to accomplish their tasks competently. The training methodology was designed in such a way to enable the participants to learn the skills and techniques of implementing regional development policies not only in purely theoretical terms but also through case examples and practical experiences. The focus of ATC was on human and institutional capacity building, which are key variables in sustainable development.

Through ATC and in-country training programmes, the Office had managed to train over 2,000 professionals. This, of course, is not a large number of trained manpower considering the large pool trained and qualified regional planners required in Africa. However, it is hoped that some of these planners, who are trained in the techniques and methodologies of training, can organize their own training programmes in their respective countries and thereby set in motion the multiplier effect.

ATC also sharpened the skills and knowledge of individual Africa planners; improved the capacity of the organizations that employ them; and increased the capacity of emerging in-country centers of excellence to mount in-country training programmes.

There are three sets of direct beneficiaries of ATC.

- The primary beneficiaries were the participants themselves. They include planners, officials, and professional staff from government ministries/agencies responsible for local and regional development and planning, and university departments and other training institutions that are engaged in research and training for local and regional development and planning. Concerted efforts were made to ensure an increased involvement of women in the to improve the gender balance in local and regional development planning and management;
- The second beneficiaries were the countries represented by the participants. Priority for participation is given to those countries emphasizing decentralization and institutionalization of local and regional planning, including Ghana in West Africa, Ethiopia and Tanzania in Eastern Africa, and Botswana, Namibia and Zimbabwe in Southern Africa.
- The third set of project beneficiaries were the local communities that participate in the ATC and the institutions involved in co-ordinating the in-country training programmes; and
- The indirect beneficiaries of the training program were the citizens of theses regions whose local governments, as a result of the project, become more responsible for addressing local requirements and desires, and more capable of delivering services and planning for the communities.

The Asia-Africa Exchange Programme of the Office was established and strengthened institutional linkages between Asian and African training, research and planning institutions and facilitated joint undertakings between policymakers, scholars and researchers of the two regions. It enhanced Africa's capacity to learn and draw lessons from Asian development experiences through cross-fertilization of ideas and experiences and laid the ground for a meaningful and effective South-South cooperation.

REFERENCES

Edralin, J. S. (1996). "Training in Regional Development Planning: The UNCRD Model" in Panganiban, E.M. (ed.) *Regional Development and HABITAT II-1996*. Nagoya: United Nations Centre for Regional Development.

Friedmann, J. (1966). *Regional Development Policy: A Case Study of Venezuela*. Cambridge, MA: MIT Press.

Gates, C. (2001). *Evaluation Report of Africa Capacity Development: The Africa Training Course on Local and Regional Development Planning and Management.* Nairobi, Kenya: UNCRD, March 2001. (Unpublished document).

John F. J. and Kumssa, A. (2008). "Training for Human Security," *Journal of Social Development in Africa* 23 (2): 9-31.

Jones, J. F. and Kumssa, A. (1996). "Distance Training in Local Social Development and the Emerging Technologies," *Social Development Issues*, 18(3):1-13.

Jones, J. F. and Yogo, T. (1994). *New Training Design for Local Social Development – The Single System Design in Competency-Based Training*. Nagoya, Japan: United Nations Centre for Regional Development.

Gruchman, B. (1981). Training of Regional Development Planners: An International Viewpoint, in Mathur, Om Prakash (E*d*.). *Training for Regional Development Planning*. Nagoya: Maruzen Asia.

Hakimian, H. and Teshome, A. (1993). *Trainers' Guide: Concepts, Principles and Methods of Training with Special Reference to Agricultural Development*. Rome: FAO.

Mabogunje, A. L. and Misra, R. P. (*Eds.)* (1981). *Regional Development Alternatives: An International Perspectives*. Nagoya, Japan: Maruzen Asia.

Misra, R. P. (1981). Development Where People Matter: Case for Comprehensive Social Policy in Mabogunje, A.L. and Misra, R.P. (*Eds*.) *Regional Development Alternatives: An International Perspectives*. Nagoya, Japan: Maruzen Asia.

Nadler, L. (1982). *Designing Training Programs: The Critical Events Model.* Reading, MA & London: Addison-Wesley Publishing Company.

Rodwin, L. (1981). Regional Planning Perspectives in Third World Countries in Mathur, Om Prakash (*Ed*.). *Training for Regional Development Planning*. Nagoya: Maruzen Asia.

INDEX

#

A

D

E

F

J

K

L

M

N

O

P

Q

Y

Z